Social Skills Success
for Students with
Autism/Asperger's

Helping Adolescents on the Spectrum to Fit In

Fred Frankel
Jeffrey J. Wood

JOSSEY-BASS
A Wiley Imprint
www.josseybass.com

KH

Published by Jossey-Bass
A Wiley Imprint
989 Market Street, San Francisco, CA 94103-1741—www.josseybass.com

Jossey-Bass books and products are available through most bookstores. To contact Jossey-Bass directly call our Customer Care Department within the U.S. at 800-956-7739, outside the U.S. at 317-572-3986, or fax 317-572-4002.

Jossey-Bass also publishes its books in a variety of electronic formats. Some content that appears in print may not be available in electronic books.

Library of Congress Cataloging-in-Publication Data
Frankel, Fred, 1946-
  Social skills success for students with autism/Asperger's : helping adolescents on the spectrum to fit in / Fred Frankel, Jeffrey J. Wood.—1st ed.
  Includes bibliographical references and index.
  ISBN 978-0-470-95238-2 (pbk.)
  ISBN 9781118108598 (ebk.)
  ISBN 9781118108604 (ebk.)
  ISBN 9781118108611 (ebk.)
  1. Youth with autism spectrum disorders—Education. 2. Youth with autism spectrum disorders—Behavior modification. 3. Social skills in adolescence. I. Wood, Jeffrey J., 1972- II. Title.
  LC4717.F465 2012
  371.94—dc23

Printed in the United States of America
FIRST EDITION
PB Printing 10 9 8 7 6 5 4 3 2 1

2/28/12

ABOUT THE AUTHORS

FRED FRANKEL, Ph.D., is professor of medical psychology in the Department of Psychiatry and Biobehavioral Sciences at the UCLA Semel Institute for Neuroscience and Human Behavior. He is the founder and director of the UCLA Parenting and Children's Friendship Program. Frankel has been principal investigator on two studies of social skills training funded by the National Institute of Mental Health (NIMH)—one grant for students with attention deficit hyperactivity disorder (ADHD) and the second for children with autism spectrum disorders. He has also been co–principal investigator on a grant funded by the Centers for Disease Control investigating social skills training for children with fetal alcohol spectrum disorders (FASD) and an NIMH-funded interdisciplinary training grant for research in childhood psychosis. He is currently a co-investigator in the Center for Autism Intervention Research Network, funded by the National Institutes of Health, and a pediatric overweight prevention grant funded by the Drown Foundation. He has published over fifty-three peer-reviewed studies on autism, ADHD, developmental disabilities, FASD, and childhood obesity. Frankel has authored three books: *Children's Friendship Training* (with Bob Myatt), *Social Skills for Teenagers with Developmental and Autism Spectrum Disorders: The PEERS Treatment Manual* (with Elizabeth Laugeson), and *Friends Forever: How Parents Can Help Their Kids Make and Keep Good Friends* (Jossey-Bass, 2010).

JEFFREY J. WOOD, Ph.D., is associate professor of education and psychiatry and biobehavioral sciences at UCLA. He developed and directs the UCLA Behavioral Interventions for Anxiety in Children with Autism (BIACA) research and treatment program. He has been principal investigator on three NIH-funded studies of cognitive behavioral therapy: one for typical students with anxiety disorders and the other two for children and adolescents with autism spectrum disorders, and principal investigator on three studies funded by Cure Autism Now, Autism Speaks, and the Organization for Autism Research investigating cognitive behavioral therapy for children and adolescents with autism spectrum disorders in school and clinic settings. He has sponsored four NIMH-funded training grants for research on child and adolescent developmental disabilities and mental health, including a school-based study of cognitive behavioral therapy for anxiety problems. He is currently principal investigator of the NICHD-funded multisite study of cognitive behavioral therapy for anxiety in adolescents with autism. He has published over thirty peer-reviewed studies on anxiety, autism, depression, and disruptive behavior disorders. Wood has authored one other book: *Child Anxiety Disorders* (with Bryce McLeod).

ACKNOWLEDGMENTS

Fred Frankel: I thank Bruce Kravetz of Palms Middle School, Los Angeles, and Cynthia Whitham, L.C.S.W., for their help in the early drafts of this book. I also acknowledge the invaluable assistance of Thomas Dase, assistant superintendent of education services of the Culver City Unified School District, for his help and support in implementing my social skills program in his school district, and Muriel Ifekwunigwe and staff at the El Rincon School Family Center.

I thank the following staff of Jossey-Bass for helping to make this book a reality: Marjorie McAneny, senior editor; Tracy Gallagher, senior editorial assistant; Robin Lloyd, production editor; Beverly Miller, copyeditor; and Dimi Berkner, senior marketing manager.

Jeffrey J. Wood: I thank my long-time collaborator, Bryce McLeod at Virginia Commonwealth University, for his extraordinary insights on anxiety issues and our ever-fascinating scholarly dialogue during the writing of this book. I am also grateful to Jeffrey Jacobs and Muriel Ifekwunigwe at the UCLA University Lab School and Angela Chiu in the UCLA Department of Psychology, with whom I collaborated on a clinical trial of cognitive behavioral therapy for youth with anxiety in a school setting.

Jossey-Bass Teacher

Jossey-Bass Teacher provides educators with practical knowledge and tools to create a positive and lifelong impact on student learning. We offer classroom-tested and research-based teaching resources for a variety of grade levels and subject areas. Whether you are an aspiring, new, or veteran teacher, we want to help you make every teaching day your best.

From ready-to-use classroom activities to the latest teaching framework, our value-packed books provide insightful, practical, and comprehensive materials on the topics that matter most to K–12 teachers. We hope to become your trusted source for the best ideas from the most experienced and respected experts in the field.

CONTENTS

To my wife, Susan, for her daily self-sacrifice to our family and support for my writing this book.
F.F.

To my first and lifelong best friend, my sister, Ann, who taught by example about what it means to be a true friend, and to my son, Jonah, for whom I wish a lifetime of friendship and happiness.
J.J.W.

INTRODUCTION

" Yes, the rule thing is pretty frustrating. I am always trying to learn THE RULE, and non-Aspie types do not seem to notice these unspoken 'rules' at all, yet they instinctively know how to behave. But I feel like there MUST be a decoding trick somewhere because I am OBVIOUSLY missing something!"

—From the blog *Life with Asperger's*

All of the chapters in this book begin with a quotation from or about an adolescent with autism. Some of these come from students we have personally worked with and others from cases we've read about. We intend for these quotations to give a more human face to the issues and interventions you will read about in the following chapters.

We are hearing more about autism and Asperger's disorder these days. In 1943, using primitive diagnostic techniques, Leo Kanner first identified a group of children with a strikingly unusual pattern of behavioral disturbances that began before they were thirty months of age. He was struck by the aloofness and repetitive stereotyped behaviors that were common among these children and labeled them as having "early infantile autism." Since then, diagnostic and research tools have become substantially more sophisticated, so that we can detect autism and Asperger's disorder in children and teens who have much milder symptoms. We are also getting better at treating these children and teens. One of the early lessons was that educational approaches are essential in this treatment and can substantially improve children's functioning. Clinicians and researchers have since determined that autism is not a unique and separate condition as once thought, but a spectrum or range of disorders, with the most severe being classic autism. Most individuals on the autism spectrum have much milder symptoms. The U.S. Centers for Disease Control estimates that the prevalence of autism spectrum disorders may be as high as 1 in 152 individuals. About 80 percent of those individuals are considered high functioning, with minimal impairments and at least average intelligence. Seven times as many males as females are affected.

Often kids with autism spectrum disorders find themselves in regular education classes. Teachers are frequently surprised by their behavior in class, yet these behavioral symptoms are often just the tip of the iceberg in terms of the difficulties with which these kids are trying to cope. They are clearly different from most other students. Teens on the autism spectrum (often referred to simply as "on the spectrum") who are included in regular education are generally able to function adequately most times. Perhaps most puzzling is the occasional meltdown, when they completely and strikingly lose control of their behavior, which is common among these kids. Regular education teachers often find these meltdowns and many other behaviors to be challenging to deal with. Special education teachers and education specialists, who are generally more aware than most regular education teachers of the problems of students with disabilities, are typically not aware of effective techniques to teach these kids how to function better.

The central deficits of autism spectrum disorders are impairments in social relations and communication (both nonverbal and verbal), together with restrictions in flexible and creative, context-sensitive thinking. Teens and tweens on the spectrum vary widely in their mental abilities and limitations, as well as in their personality and sociability. Most have average or above-average intelligence. Although individuals vary on the symptoms they have, in most cases they continue to experience significant impairment in social and vocational functioning after graduation from high school. Students on the spectrum have profound difficulties in relating to their peers, regardless of their level of cognitive ability, and these difficulties place them at significant risk for developing other behavioral and emotional difficulties such as anxiety.

Kids on the spectrum will not learn how to have more meaningful social relationships simply by watching other people or participating in various social situations. They don't seem to have guiding principles as to how to acquire the social knowledge they need. Nevertheless, they are very motivated to learn, and the interventions we have conducted in our research and outpatient clinic programs have shown us that students on the spectrum can indeed learn social interaction and self-regulation skills. These kids are enjoyable to work with: they are usually eager to learn skills that help them fit in and have few defenses to get in the way of learning. They don't hide their emotions or lie about their feelings.

Our Approach to Social Skills Training

Our approach to social skills training has been to identify key common social situations and teach the social etiquette as a series of simple rules to follow. This is an easy way for tweens and teens to understand how to fit in based on social context. Structuring social behavior in terms of critical situations and accompanying rules of etiquette for each requires minimal consideration of the viewpoints of others and abstract thinking on the part of the tweens and teens on the spectrum.

Consider the etiquette that has evolved around ATM machines. Such machines are relatively new. When faced with this novel situation some years ago, considerate people began to apply the golden rule (do unto others as you would have them do unto you). They wanted to make others as comfortable as possible about personal space and also make it clear that they were not looking at the ATM screen when others were entering passwords to withdraw money. So they lined up as in other situations, but kept a distance of four or five feet between the person using the machine and the next in line. This is close enough to signal they are in line but far enough away to maintain the privacy of the person using the machine. Soon everyone began to do this in front of ATM machines.

The Knowledge Base Behind This Book

This book is based on techniques we've developed in the fields of social skills instruction and emotion regulation. These techniques have been found to be successful in helping students on the spectrum.

Children's Friendship Training/PEERS

Fred Frankel has published two treatment manuals that have been tested in studies and found to help. *Children's Friendship Training,* coauthored with Bob Myatt, describes in detail twelve sessions devoted to training conversational skills, other skills to allow children and early teens (up to sixth graders) to meet new friends, and how parents and children can collaborate to have a parent-supervised play date. The *PEERS Treatment Manual,* written with Elizabeth Laugeson, extends this program to teens in middle and high school. Both interventions are designed to take place in an outpatient setting using concurrent student and parent weekly one-hour sessions over three months.

Both programs are compatible with school-based interventions, such as those described in this book. Results of clinical trials at the University of California, Los Angeles, on both interventions showed that students on the spectrum increased their numbers of monthly get-togethers from a baseline level of typically none to two to three per month at the end of treatment. Our three-year follow-up study of thirty-three teens and sixty-eight children (with the expected amount of sample attrition over the three years) revealed that students continued to have get-togethers at the frequency we noted immediately after treatment stopped. The most gratifying finding was that three years after the end of treatment, these get-togethers were reciprocated by their friends with equal frequency.

Frankel has successfully implemented children's friendship training as an after-school program in the Culver City, California, schools. He has also helped professionals in a private clinic to implement PEERS in the Seattle, Washington, public schools.

The unique features of children's friendship training are as follows:

- Parent participation is an integral part of the intervention.

- Homework assignments are part of every treatment session.

- Skills that have been shown to contribute to social competence in typically developing (that is, neurotypical) peers (those off the autism spectrum) are taught to group members.

- Parents and children work together to host get-togethers. Having enjoyable play dates promotes best friendships.

- Teaching tactful methods in handling being teased in order to gain sympathy from bystanders.

The PEERS intervention contains all of these features. In addition, modules have been designed to address social issues specific to teens with autism spectrum disorders:

- Identification of appropriate crowds for the teen (members of these crowds may call themselves the jocks, the band crowd, or computer geeks). The teen is then coached on how to join in conversations that peers in these crowds are having, for example, in the school lunchroom.

- Teaching teens how to gracefully exit a conversation after choosing the wrong peers.

- Distinguishing between teasing and embarrassing feedback (for instance, about poor grooming and hygiene).

- Teaching teens how to organize a get-together.

- Teaching rules for electronic communication, including phone etiquette, and rules of text messaging, instant messaging, and e-mailing, in which the teens may unknowingly "harass" others.

Although this book is focused on helping kids on the spectrum fit into middle and high school life, the PEERS manual helps them primarily with the social skills they need after school in order to develop best friendships. We refer in this book to the relevant modules of the PEERS manual that will enhance the school experience of teens on the spectrum.

Cognitive-Behavioral Strategies for Emotional Self-Regulation

Jeffrey Wood has developed techniques to help students on the spectrum with emotional self-regulation. Students who lack skills to manage their anxiety are prone to outbursts and meltdowns in school, which jeopardizes their ability to make and maintain positive peer relationships and interferes with their academic achievement. Wood has developed three treatment manuals to address anxiety and related emotional problems: one for neurotypical children and two for children and teens on the autism spectrum. Multiple research studies have shown that these interventions are effective in increasing emotional self-control, decreasing behavioral symptoms, and improving the social adjustment of youth on and off the spectrum. About 70 percent of participants in these treatments no longer have an anxiety disorder diagnosis after completing the treatment. Wood's follow-up studies show that these improvements are maintained at least one year after the end of the intervention. The interventions, designed for and tested in both school and outpatient clinic settings, typically have involved about twelve to sixteen weekly ninety-minute sessions. Parent involvement and homework assignments are an integral aspect of each version of the anxiety program.

The unique features of the anxiety management program are as follows:

- Emotion recognition skills are taught using multimodal teaching: incorporating class discussions, visual supports, role-playing, and writing. Examples are used that are interesting and motivating to teens on the spectrum in order to enhance their understanding of the material and their level of participation.

- Teens learn basic psychological principles of thought recognition and thought modification as a means of coping with anxiety and distress. These are core skills for individuals who are able to manage their emotions effectively.

- The universal principle of facing fear to fight fear is taught and practiced in multiple ways that encourage continuous success, engagement, and mastery of challenging situations over the course of the intervention.

- Parents and teachers are given tools to promote student participation in the anxiety program and use of the skills in the classroom and at home.

This training program, adapted for use in schools, is presented in Chapters Nine and Ten of this book.

The Purpose of This Book

This book is directed to teachers and special educators working with high-functioning adolescents on the spectrum who are in special education settings or partially or fully included in regular education classes. Parents of tweens and teens on the spectrum often have to take on the advocacy role in the absence of services. Thus, parents may be interested in this book as a resource for their child's teachers.

This book helps teachers recognize the social problems of these adolescents, educates teachers as to what they need to know about autism spectrum disorders, discusses the advantages and disadvantages of different school options for these students, and gives them brief classroom interventions they can use to remedy social problems without further stigmatizing the teens. The book has three main purposes:

1. To provide teachers with a better understanding of students on the spectrum

2. To provide teachers with the tools to help these youngsters fit in better with peers, so that they are better able to be integrated into the academic life of students in middle and high school

3. To give school personnel an understanding of and tools to use with teens on the spectrum who have anxiety and meltdowns

Our approach is to teach the kids how to handle their anxiety so that they avoid meltdowns and provide them with skills to be better integrated into their school environment. In the long run, this is a more beneficial approach than adjusting their environment to accommodate their symptoms.

There are different levels of peer acceptance. At the lowest level, it involves a willingness to tolerate and associate with the student on the spectrum for purposes of school assignments. A higher level is characterized by respect for the tween and teen as an individual. Neither of these levels involves what we might consider friendships. The next higher level is that of accepting a kid into a crowd. The highest level is maintaining a mutual best friendship. Since this book is aimed at informing teachers how best to help students on the spectrum participate more fully in school life, we focus primarily on the first two levels of acceptance and touch on the highest levels insofar as teachers can help in these areas.

The lack of peer acceptance can have indirect effects on academic achievement. When kids face peer rejection, neglect, or sometimes even abuse and bullying, they may develop anxiety and depression that, among other things, undermines their motivation to focus on school work. When peers avoid and isolate the student on the spectrum from classroom participation, these young people are at a distinct disadvantage in completing assignments. Students on the spectrum who know how to fit in with peers can gain increased help in academic and social areas of life.

How to Use This Book

As a convenience for purposes of this book, we refer to students with any of the autism spectrum disorders as either "on the spectrum" or "students with autism spectrum disorder." This includes those having classic autism who are high functioning, those with Asperger's syndrome, those with pervasive developmental disorders, and those who are frequently referred to in the popular literature as having nonverbal learning disorders. In case examples and elsewhere, we refer to students as "he" for simplicity of presentation, but recognizing that we are also including girls on the spectrum. We are focusing on students in grades 6 to 12—tweens and teens alike. However, for simplicity, we use the term *teen*.

This book is divided into three major parts. The emphasis in Part One is on providing a deeper level of understanding of the challenges to adolescents on the spectrum. We provide a review of developmental issues facing all teens that are important for a better understanding of kids on the spectrum. Chapter One describes how teachers are likely to encounter the symptoms of autism spectrum disorders in their students and offers helpful advice for how to address some of the minor symptoms. Chapter Two reviews different options for educational placement for teens on the spectrum. We provide a lesson plan to help the school community, including possible peer mentors, better understand and help students with autism spectrum disorders. Chapter Three reviews tips for classroom management for kids who are in segregated, partially, and fully included classroom situations, as well as how to have teachers start formal social skill training programs.

Part Two describes brief interventions that will help teens on the spectrum better integrate into the social fabric of middle and high school. The interventions offered in this part are short and focused. Chapter Four helps kids expand their interests and after-school activities so that they are more likely to fit in with their peer group. Chapter Five improves comprehension of nonliteral language (idioms and sarcasm). Chapter Six addresses increasing adolescents' skills for understanding conversations. Chapter Seven improves social conversation by teaching teens on the spectrum to use small talk as a way of cautiously approaching peers for friendship overtures and by helping teens on the spectrum identify and use the parts of a conversation. Chapter Eight provides teachers guidelines for helping students on the spectrum select appropriate peers to eventually be closer friends.

Part Three presents more extensive interventions that have a broader impact. Chapter Nine focuses on understanding and assessing the sources of anxiety that concern kids on the spectrum. Chapter Ten describes an effective intervention for anxiety-related responses that may stigmatize teens. Chapter Eleven presents individual and whole-school approaches to prevent and deal with victimization. Chapter Twelve offers an approach for peer mentoring and coaching that has proven effective in helping kids fit in.

We hope that readers will find that students on the spectrum and their neurotypical peers will have a more rewarding school experience as a result of trying the lessons we present in this book.

PART ONE

BASIC INFORMATION ABOUT TEENS WITH AUTISM SPECTRUM DISORDER

CHAPTER 1

What Is Autism Spectrum Disorder?

> *Leon was the youngest of three boys born to a mother who was a surgeon and a father who was an engineer. His older two brothers excelled in basketball and soccer, but he was awkward and uncoordinated and consequently hated all sports. Starting in elementary school, Leon's primary interest was street maps. He spent recess and lunch alone reading maps. At home he had no play dates and often spent his playtime looking over local street maps with his parents. He had memorized all of the local streets. On beginning a car ride, he would inquire as to the destination and then proceed to give accurate directions.*
>
> *By middle school, he was still an elementary school child in many ways. He didn't care about the clothes and fads that captivated his peers. He wouldn't comb his hair or brush his teeth in the morning, and he wore the same clothes as he had in elementary school. Some were torn and worn out, but he liked wearing them because they were comfortable. His favorite game was playing with small plastic blocks. He had a Facebook page that featured his two hamsters.*

The teenage years offer many new challenges for parents. Exasperated parents often say that their experiences with their teens make it easier for them to allow their children to eventually leave home to become more independent. Some of the difficulties adults face with adolescents on the spectrum stem from the fact that they are teens. Thus, in order to better understand adolescents on the spectrum, we also need to understand the context and issues facing all tweens and teens.

Challenges Facing Neurotypical Teens

In order to be better adjusted, not only as teens but later as adults, these students must master five challenges. Many middle and high school teachers are aware of these, but we summarize them in order to expand on how they affect the adolescent on the spectrum.

Becoming Independent from Parents

Teens become increasingly more involved with and dependent on their peers. One study of teen time use found that teens spend more time with their peers (mean was 449 minutes per day) than with their parents (mean was 248 minutes per day, mostly watching TV together) or alone (241 minutes per day). Looking across all of the teens in the study, the investigators found that the teenage boys who spent more time with their parents did so at the expense of their alone time. The teenage girls who spent more time with their parents did so at the expense of their peers. Thus, time with parents seems to detract more from the social lives of girls than from those of boys.

At the same time they become more dependent on peers, teens are pulling away from their parents. Family relationships of teens are stormier than those of younger children. Predictably, most of the conflict centers on the teens' striving for greater autonomy. The typical teen averages about two conflicts (with everyone) every three days. Perhaps because they are usually more involved in child rearing, mothers are involved in more of these arguments than fathers. As a consequence of more conflict, teens' affection and helpfulness toward parents decline.

Although some adolescents on the spectrum are more docile and child-like than their neurotypical peers, many become surlier and act out more, especially toward parents. Many become less willing to accept help and advice from their parents. The adolescents on the spectrum who are more effective in their struggle for autonomy may seem more problematic for parents. The problem with these teens' striving for autonomy is that their parents usually perceive that they aren't adequately equipped to handle much of what greater autonomy brings. They perceive their teens on the spectrum as needing more specific help with life challenges than do neurotypical teens.

As the saying goes, "No man is an island." We should all know our limitations and learn when to ask for help, from whom, and how. Teens' deteriorating relationships with their parents often mean that they rarely ask them for help and guidance. More than ever before, it's helpful for these young people to have someone such as a trusted teacher, older peer mentor, or guidance counselor to fill this void. They are more likely to welcome guidance and information if it comes from a trusted adult *other than a parent*. In Chapter Twelve, we propose that a slightly older peer mentor can also help in this regard.

Preparing for a Vocation or Career

Vocational counselors use two kinds of assessments to help people select potential careers. One is to assess their range of interests and skills and try to fit them to careers where their skills would be most useful. Another type of assessment is based on the people with whom they like to associate. Young adults form many of their relationships with others at their job, and these relationships generally help to improve their job performance and job satisfaction. Relationship impairments of adolescents on the spectrum are thus limiting to their eventual job placement, satisfaction, and performance on the job.

Teens on the spectrum may at least partially grow out of some of their symptoms. They may have had a narrowly restricted range of interests as children but are now ready to expand those. Our experience has been that students on the spectrum are able to widen their range as long as their anxiety doesn't get in the way. Chapter Four addresses how to increase the range of their interests, which will be helpful in terms of eventual job and friend choice.

Adjusting to the Physical and Psychosexual Changes of Puberty

Not only is the social landscape changing for teens, but so are their bodies. Teens on the spectrum are generally unprepared to meet the challenges of sexuality and romance. The more docile and childlike tweens and teens on the spectrum may be oblivious to these issues. Many want a girlfriend or boyfriend, but just as characteristic of their social interactions with peers in general, they are clueless about what having a romantic relationship entails. Boys on the spectrum may be especially at risk for accusations of harassment or, worse, stalking. Girls on the spectrum are especially at risk for being exploited or, worse, becoming victims. Chapter Eleven deals with issues of victimization more fully.

Developing Values and Identity

Teens require a lot of time to process the changes that are taking place in their lives. One study, using electronic pagers to prompt teens to report what they were doing and their emotional states throughout the week, reported that neurotypical teens spend an average of about 25 percent of their waking hours in solitude, mostly of their choice. This solitude is ben-eficial to them: those who spent between 30 and 40 percent of their waking hours alone had better grade point averages than students spending either more or less time alone. They were also rated as better adjusted by their teachers and peers. Thus, adolescents on the spectrum may require some amount of solitude, mainly at home, in order to process their life challenges and changes much as neurotypical teens do.

Establishing Effective Relationships with Peers

Early conceptions of individuals with autism characterized them as having a powerful desire for aloneness. We have observed that rather than wanting to be alone more than other teens do, high-functioning teens on the spectrum want to be more like the teens they see around them, but they don't know how to engage their peers effectively. Many cannot form even superficial friend-ships, and most cannot become more intimate with the friends they have.

Students on the spectrum are aware of being socially rejected. Only 27 percent reported having a best friend while this applied to 41 percent of students with other developmental disabilities. Many teens on the spectrum have a limited knowledge of what a friend is. For example, they may say they have one or two friends but can't remember their names. They may name others they occasionally see at school but never get together with them outside school. They report having poorer relationships and less satisfying companionship with the friends they may have, as well as more loneliness at school, compared with neurotypical peers.

These teens' continued isolation makes deficits in the knowledge of peer etiquette more obvious as they get older. As adults, many individuals on the spectrum lack community connections and friendships that neurotypical persons take for granted. For these reasons, the PEERS intervention instructs kids on the qualities of friendships and teaches them the steps to join crowds and make best friends.

Neurotypical teens are able to establish relationships at many levels, which can be categorized as their crowd, their friends, and their very best friends. Kids seek out others like themselves and become more like those they associate with. Friends are similar to each other on demographics, school-related attitudes and attitudes about teen culture (smoking, drinking, drug use, dating, and participation in religious activities), dress, and grooming. All of these factors are concretized in the "crowd." The crowd is a unique category of looser friendships that emerges in adolescence, and each crowd is described by a name—for example, the Jocks, Brains, Burnouts, Computer Geeks, Rednecks, and Goths.

Within the crowd, teens form cliques with four or so other teens. Unlike the cliques in elementary school, mixed-gender cliques sometimes form at this stage, and these groups tend to be stable. Whereas elementary school friendships weaken when the children are assigned to different classrooms at the beginning of each school year, middle and high school cliques are stable across years and over the summer since teens are able to travel to each other's houses and meet in different locations without much parent involvement.

Despite the crowd's importance in the process of defining teen identity, it has been largely overlooked by clinicians who are training teens in social skills, largely forgotten by parents of kids on the spectrum, and largely ignored by the teens on the spectrum themselves, often at their social peril. For example, a teen on the spectrum with limited musical ability may try to join the band crowd. As our experiences with the PEERS intervention have shown us, it is very useful to teach teens (and remind their parents) about this social feature. The roles that teachers can play in this are discussed more fully in Chapter Eight.

Most teens have one or two best friends they see daily. Psychological sharing (intimacy) is an important part of many teen friendships, especially for girls, who tend to have a greater number of intimate friends than boys do. Many neurotypical boys have poor-quality friendships that are competitive rather than intimate. Reflecting this, the referral rate to social skills groups for neurotypical students is three times greater for boys than girls.

Symptoms of Autism Spectrum Disorders

Not only do teens on the spectrum face challenges of adolescence, they have additional challenges due to their symptoms of autism. A review of the symptoms of autism spectrum disorders leads to an appreciation of how much research went into uncovering the core symptoms of these disorders and how difficult diagnosis can be. In fact, there is no adequate description of a "typical teen on the spectrum." These students are individuals just like everyone else. A given teen on the spectrum may not show any particular symptom. Also the severity of symptoms differs widely among teens.

Many of the social problems of teens on the spectrum can be ascribed to misleading teachers into thinking that these teens know more than they actually do, deficits in expressing themselves to others, deficits in understanding others, and coping with anxiety-provoking situations. We now explore these symptoms, identifying those that have a higher need to be addressed and those that seem less central to social adjustment. Where appropriate, we suggest simple interventions or identify the chapters in this book that address them.

Misleading Aspects of Communication

Several features of the autism spectrum disorders not only mask deficits but create a false impression of age-appropriate or advanced skills. Students on the spectrum seem quite verbal. Their detail-oriented, overly formal style of expressing themselves with advanced vocabularies may give the impression that they understand more than they actually do.

Teens on the spectrum are sometimes described as having nonverbal learning disabilities. Yet on standardized IQ tests, their scores are generally similar in verbal and nonverbal areas to those of their neurotypical peers. In contrast, they show relatively poor performance on verbal skills such as social judgment and understanding of social conventions. They tend to have good rote memory skills and good comprehension of factual material, leading many teachers to think that they are quite intelligent in a broader sense. However, this can be very misleading. Higher expectations that arise from this false impression can be stressful for both teachers and the teens.

Deficits in Expression and Communication

We communicate not only with words but through our gestures and facial expressions as we speak. We also sometimes hide our true intent in a conversation so as not to make our listeners uncomfortable. Tweens and teens on the spectrum miss many of these conversational nuances.

NONVERBAL ASPECTS OF COMMUNICATION

Teens on the spectrum may fail to use nonverbal aspects of communication. They show very little body language, maintain too little or too much social distance from their listener, and have flat or unusual voice pitch variation and inflection. Perhaps the most stigmatizing aspect, because it causes discomfort in listeners, is social distance. This is fairly easy to correct: the rule of etiquette is to stay about an arm's length from your listener (and refrain from measuring it with your arms). Following this rule will handle many social situations.

Also, kids on the spectrum do not generally show their distress through voice tone or other nonverbal cues, so that a difficult situation can escalate substantially before others are aware of their difficulties. We have found that teaching teens on the spectrum how to recognize their own anxiety helps them reduce their anxiety and prevent eventual meltdowns. Chapter Ten presents this approach in more detail.

SOCIAL ASPECTS OF COMMUNICATION

Students on the spectrum miss the more formal parts of conversations: introductions and excuses we make for starting and ending conversations so that conversational flow is less abrupt (sometimes we refer to these as "cover stories"). They will miss the point of the short "How are you?" exchange, often going on too long. They can be quite blunt in their communications, which others often misinterpret as rudeness. Chapters Six and Seven deal with how to remediate these kinds of issues.

Adolescents on the spectrum are noted to have poor eye contact during social conversations. Much research has shown that lower-functioning individuals on the spectrum have unusual patterns of visually scanning their environment. Neurotypical males have poorer eye contact in conversations than neurotypical females do. However, high-functioning teens on the spectrum, being mostly males (there are seven times as many boys on the spectrum as there are girls), usually do not show glaring differences from other males in social eye contact during conversations. Furthermore, teaching teen boys to give eye contact to other teen boys will more likely make the other teen boys feel uncomfortable.

COGNITIVE RIGIDITY.   Many teens on the spectrum like everything to be the same and everything to be in what they view as the right place. They can get very upset and are sure to point out if something is done in what they consider 'the wrong way', especially in regard to their focal interest, if they have one. They are the rules and syllabus police. For some teens on the spectrum, this is expressed in little variation in the clothing they wear. One teen we know preferred to wear a neat white shirt with a pocket protector for pencils and no ridges on his collar every day he came to school. Although these kids are poor at setting up routines for efficient self-organization, they may rigidly follow their routine in exactly the same way every day. Thus, any changes in school routines may be especially challenging for them. They benefit greatly by being warned in advance and specifically how things in their routines are about to change (for example, at the end of the school year or the start of a new one) and will need very specific help on managing the change.

On the other hand, many teens on the spectrum may have had a narrowly restricted range of interests as children but are now ready to expand their interests. Our experience has been that these adolescents are able to widen their range as long as their anxiety doesn't get in the way. Chapter Four addresses this problem.

HUMOR PRODUCTION.   As a device used for making and keeping friends, research suggests that telling jokes tends to impair the development of friendship. One research study of a two-month summer camp classified neurotypical preteens into three main groups based on friendships throughout the camp. One group acquired and maintained the same friends, another group never acquired friends, and the third group went through friends quickly, having different friends at the end of the camp experience than at the beginning. Children in this last group, classified as the second most problematic one (next to the group that never acquired friends), were characterized more by telling funny jokes. They were able to make new friends, but apparently their friends tired of their jokes and moved on, to be replaced by a fresh group of new friends in the end.

Most kids on the spectrum have difficulty with both understanding the humor of others and delivering their own jokes. Their humor tends to be more indicative of much younger children (one study found that adults on the spectrum told jokes more indicative of preschoolers). Only 16 percent of adults on the spectrum could tell jokes that were age appropriate for teens and adults. When asked to pick funny punch lines for jokes in one study, teens on the spectrum tended to pick punch lines that were unrelated to the content of jokes or picked straightforward endings that were not humorous at all. For these reasons, joke telling tends to further stigmatize most kids on the spectrum and should be discouraged in most cases.

Our major thrust during PEERS social skills intervention has been to evaluate whether individual teens on the spectrum are capable of telling jokes in a way that does not further stigmatize them. A relatively few individuals could do so, and so they had no intervention. For the many who couldn't, we tried to have them give up being joke tellers by focusing instead on glorifying the role of the joke receiver, emphasizing the vital role of the joke receiver in joke delivery.

CONVERSATIONAL REPAIR PROCESSES.

Teens on the spectrum are generally better at engaging in online or written conversations than oral conversations. This is because they have time to more fully process what has been said in a written conversation, while the content of oral conversations is not as available after it has been said and the listener is under pressure to respond more quickly than in a written conversation. Neurotypical teens have skills to ensure that they understand what has transpired, and they use these skills to "repair" the conversation to full comprehension. In contrast, teens on the spectrum may know they missed something but lack repair skills. Teaching conversational repair processes are part of Chapter Six.

IMPROVING SOCIAL CONVERSATION.   Kids on the spectrum can be taught to improve their social conversations. For instance, these teens are not thought to be aware of what interests their peers. However, when they are taught how to find common interests with potential friends as part of the PEERS intervention, they quickly learned how to have this conversation and learned what interests they had in common with potential friends.

Easily Corrected Deficits in Understanding Others

Some of the most important deficits that students on the spectrum have can be corrected with simple instructional techniques.

THEORY OF MIND

Theory of mind is the ability to recognize emotions and infer what others are thinking or intending from their voice tone, facial gestures, or behavior. Teens on the spectrum have difficulties with all of these aspects of theory of mind. They differ significantly from age-mates, and they don't seem to grow out of these deficits. There have been several successful studies on training children on the spectrum to be more proficient in theory of mind, but so far, none have demonstrated improvement in peer relationships. Nor have there been any studies suggesting a central role in these abilities in peer relationships for neurotypical teens. This is quite puzzling but suggests that such instruction should receive a low priority until we understand how it may help.

NONLITERAL AND VAGUE LANGUAGE

Most neurotypical people know that people sometimes don't mean what they literally seem to be saying. This arises in everyday speech when the speaker uses an idiom or employs irony or sarcasm. We can detect sarcasm at very young ages and by adolescence are masters of it. We have knowledge of certain phrases (for example, slang and idioms) and automatically translate them into their actual meaning. Students on the spectrum have difficulty understanding nonliteral language. If you tell a teen on the spectrum to "let sleeping dogs lie," they are likely to ask where the dog is.

This deficit can be addressed quite simply. Non-English speakers have similar problems when they are learning English, since foreign languages rarely have the same idioms. They are taught what the most commonly used idioms mean. Similarly, teens on the spectrum can be taught an expanded list of commonly used idioms. With continued training, they can begin to identify idioms they don't understand and develop skills to learn these idioms as they come up in conversations. We discuss comprehension of sarcasm, irony, idioms, and slang more fully in Chapter Five.

Perhaps related to their difficulties with nonliteral language, teens on the spectrum have difficulty interpreting vague requests, such as, "Come back later." Stories abound of how they come back repeatedly until the speaker is exasperated or finally says something more definite, such as, "Come back in fifteen minutes." This also can be remedied with a conversational repair, such as politely asking, "When would be a good time to come back?" The speaker may find this slightly annoying but not nearly as annoying as someone who comes back repeatedly.

Conversational repair processes thus can be thought of as on-the-fly social learning because they teach kids to recognize their limitations, make an appropriate statement that may lessen the impact of their social faux pas at the moment, and help them correct their behavior in the future.

HUMOR COMPREHENSION

Humor is a special category of nonliteral language, since it often counts on the listener's initially making a literal interpretation in an ambiguous situation. A joke punch line often has a surprise ending based on a seemingly normal course of events described in the rest of the joke, and comprehension rests on realizing that it can be interpreted in more than one way. The listener must then reevaluate the first part of the joke. Individuals on the spectrum seem to have particular deficits in this ability. Verbal IQ does not seem to be a predictor of these teens' ability to comprehend humor.

The appreciation of humorous communication is not a necessary part of human social behavior, but it sometimes makes uncomfortable situations more bearable. Many people who are not on the spectrum have what is commonly referred to as a poor sense of humor. It doesn't seem to impair their overall social adjustment, however. In fact, people will avoid telling them jokes so that they are exposed less to their areas of deficit. Deficits in humor appreciation become a problem only if the teen on the spectrum asks persistent questions about a joke. If he or she notices that others are laughing, that could be the cue not to ask such questions.

Coping with Anxiety-Producing Situations

A complete approach to the social problems in students with autism spectrum disorders is to address both their skill deficits and their anxiety. Approximately 50 to 75 percent of tweens and teens on the spectrum have an anxiety disorder. In many cases, their anxiety worsens over adolescence as they face increasingly complex social demands. Teachers are more likely to notice anxiety and depression in kids on the spectrum than are their parents. This is consistent with teens' feeling more anxious in school environments, when around peers or in academically demanding situations, than in the relatively accepting home environment.

As we discuss further in Chapter Nine, teens on the spectrum are likely to have any one of several types of anxiety disorders that diagnosticians have identified. Studies report that students on the spectrum are more likely to have an anxiety disorder than neurotypical teens and teens with other developmental disabilities. In general, the more likely a teen with autism spectrum disorders is to be aware of his social challenges, the more likely he is to have an anxiety disorder. For example, individuals on the spectrum with higher IQ were found to experience the most severe anxiety. Those on the spectrum with very poor social skills, and consequently no friends, experienced less anxiety than those with limited friendships.

Many teens on the spectrum have social anxiety, which contributes to their avoidance of social situations and awkward interactions with peers; of course, this avoidance only increases their isolation from their peers. Surveys of parents of adolescents on the spectrum report that this anxiety can lead to conduct problems, meltdowns, sensory hypersensitivity, and inattention. The phenomenon of sensory overload has been frequently described as part of a meltdown. Chapter Ten presents an effective cognitive behavioral treatment that has been tested within the school environment.

People with poor social skills compound their problems by giving the impression that they don't want to know what they're doing to make others uncomfortable and won't try to correct their mistakes. Teens on the spectrum who make the best adjustments are those who know their own strengths and weaknesses, which they try to correct. In this chapter, we have reviewed the most important social deficits that teens on the spectrum may have and in the remaining chapters of this book explore how to address these.

KEY FEATURES AND HELPFUL HINTS FOR ADOLESCENTS ON THE AUTISM SPECTRUM

- The formal and detail-oriented language of teens on the spectrum creates a false impression of broad intelligence. Their actual aptitudes may be confined to memorization of factual material.
- They have difficulty comprehending vague requests, such as, "Come back later." Teach the tween or teen to ask when a good time would be to return.
- They may stand either too close or too far away in conversation and benefit greatly from being told to stand at arm's distance from listeners.
- They will miss the point of the short "How are you?" exchange, often going on too long. They need to be taught how to use and understand this type of conversation. (See Chapter Seven.)
- They are strongly tied to routines and benefit greatly when being told in detail and in advance of impending changes in routines and will need specific help on how to manage the change.
- They have difficulty maintaining comprehension of a conversation. They should be taught how to feel comfortable in asking questions about parts of a conversation they don't understand. When comprehension breaks down, they need to be taught to use "repair processes" to restore comprehension. (See Chapter Six.)
- Teens on the spectrum often have trouble understanding idioms, irony, sarcasm, slang, and other "nonliteral" aspects of language. They need to be taught how to identify them in conversations and how to find out their meaning. (See Chapter Five.)
- Many kids on the spectrum who are partially or fully included seek to be part of the mainstream social life of their school and are aware when they are ostracized.
- Many teens on the spectrum may have to learn to fit in with a suitable crowd. (See Chapter Eight.)
- Some kids on the spectrum are not as inclined to follow parent advice as in the past and may benefit from guidance from a slightly older peer mentor about grooming and hygiene. (See Chapter Twelve.)

- In most cases, they have difficulty in both understanding humor (unless it is slapstick) and telling age-appropriate jokes. Thus, they should be discouraged from joke telling .
- The chances are 50 to 75 percent that a high-functioning teen on the spectrum will have an anxiety disorder. Sensory overload seems to be part of the experiences that teens on the spectrum have when they are having an anxiety attack. (See Chapter Nine.)
- The lack of use of voice tone and body language by students on the spectrum to convey their feelings means that they cannot easily communicate stress and anxiety until a situation escalates to a meltdown. (See Chapter Ten.)
- Some adolescents on the spectrum may need a place to calm down and collect themselves when they are becoming anxious. (See Chapter Ten.)

CHAPTER 2

Making Inclusion More Successful for Students with Autism

> " *Being an Aspie has been hard for me. I look either very smart or age appropriate most of the time. I grew up hearing, 'Stop acting like a [child much younger than me].' It really hurts my self-esteem. If I ask questions, people might think I'm joking because how could anyone fail to understand what they mean? I might sometimes want my parents' help, but I resent their getting involved. If I tell people I have Asperger's, people don't think I really have it. They say I'm just trying to excuse my behavior because, after all, I seem basically normal.* "

Many students on the spectrum wake up socially when they reach middle school. It is often surprising to see how a child with lots of symptoms progresses after a few years to a teen with fewer and subtler symptoms and a growing awareness of his peer environment. Part of this is due to the student's continuing to acquire cognitive capacity and the decrease of their symptoms. Part of this may be a function of the types of educational placements they have had in elementary school. There is a delicate balance between providing enough services in order to have each student reach his full potential and providing either too restrictive an environment so that progress is slowed or too inclusive an environment so that the student experiences academic or social setbacks.

In order to present a clearer picture of the forces at play and the effects on the student on the spectrum, we first briefly review how we came to our current philosophy of inclusion and the types of options that have been employed in the educational history of teens on the spectrum. We also review the impact of these options on parents of kids on the spectrum and regular education teachers. Finally we offer some guidelines and a lesson plan to improve the integration of teens on the spectrum with neurotypical teens.

History of the Inclusion Movement

The move toward mainstreaming began in the 1960s for children with developmental disabilities. Research at that time showed that children with milder disabilities have higher academic achievement when they are placed in regular education classes than when placed in special education classes. The research also showed that this came at the price of social acceptance by their peers. These students were more socially accepted in special education classes by their developmentally disabled peers than they were in regular education classes by average- and above-average-achieving peers. As with many other studies on groups of individuals, however, the results didn't apply to every individual in the group. Many children labeled as developmentally delayed had little or no social impairment and easily made the transition to regular classes.

Parents of children with autism spectrum disorders have fought for inclusion into general education classrooms, which they believe will improve their child's social functioning and help keep their child on a path toward higher education. Since the early 1990s, there has been an increased push toward inclusion of children, and inclusion of these students is increasingly common today.

Many parents identify the exposure to neurotypical peers as the major motivating factor in having their children in inclusive school settings and increasingly prefer partial or full inclusion of their children. Many professionals believe that placing children with autism spectrum disorders in general educational settings increases the involvement of these children in the mainstream of society through improving the children's social behavior repertoires and society's acceptance and appreciation of people with differences. Individual stories indicate that with adequate support and accommodations, some students with autism spectrum disorders can be successful in school. And in fact, substantial numbers go on to college.

Individual schools and school districts interpret the principle of inclusion in a variety of ways. What is full inclusion? Should all students with disabilities be full members of the general education classroom? If not, how much time should they be there?

Parent Views About Inclusion

There is considerable self-selection in studies that assess parent satisfaction with class placement, and many children are placed where their parents want them to be. Not surprisingly, one study found that parents whose children were in inclusive settings preferred inclusion, while parents whose children were in special schools preferred this setting. Many parents were in favor of the idea of inclusive education but expressed worries about safety, attitudes of other students (including possible verbal and physical abuse by peers and social isolation), staff and program quality, lack of appropriate support, and potential for academic failure.

Types of Educational Placement

Alternative educational placements for students with autism spectrum disorders range from the segregated special education school or classroom on a regular education campus to full inclusion in a regular education class.

The least inclusive alternative, the special education school or classroom on a regular school campus, offers several distinct advantages over other alternatives. Teachers are usually trained with the additional skills necessary to assess the individual needs of each special student. The classes are small, so that teachers usually have the time to devote to fulfilling the needs of each student. They have the training and the time to understand the emotional needs of each student and can help each student feel accepted by classmates. This setting is especially helpful for many students who have more severe symptoms of autism spectrum disorders. Some students with autism spectrum disorders may prefer to be in this placement because they are not singled out and may feel more comfortable and accepted for who they are among their peers and by the teacher.

Nevertheless, this option has disadvantages:

- Although a special education class is somewhat of a protected environment, it doesn't shield students from teasing and bullying.

- Students have minimal interaction with neurotypical students on the same campus.

- A stigma is associated with students from special education classes among neurotypical students when they integrate into such places as common lunchrooms.

Several partial inclusion alternatives have been employed, varying in the amount of pullout time between regular and special classrooms. They vary from having a single regular education class for a student primarily in special education classes to having resource room support for one or two subjects for a student primarily in regular education classes. The single regular education class alternative is often used to test the waters for a more complete transition into regular education. However, this placement makes it difficult for students on the spectrum to establish relationships with neurotypical peers, since the students go back into the special education classroom and are out of circulation with neurotypical classmates for the rest of the day.

A very common and growing practice, usually for elementary school students who cannot yet function independently, is to assign the student with autism spectrum disorders an aide, or "shadow," at school. As the term implies, this individual shadows a child at school in order to support the child in social situations during the school day. Some act as general classroom aides and only occasionally help the student with autism spectrum disorders. Some follow the student only during play activities, and some are with them the entire day. Rarely are shadows given any specific information or training as to how to help their assigned student with social integration. Nevertheless, some counseling programs include instruction for shadows as part of their services and frequent meetings with shadows to fine-tune the intervention based on a student's current needs.

Research studies provide no support for the practice of shadowing. Furthermore, interviews with students with autism spectrum disorders who had aides when they were younger say that this practice marked them as being different and therefore usually interfered with rather than facilitated their peer relationships. Thus, if shadows are not part of a social skills intervention or do not receive supervision from a knowledgeable professional, they may impede rather than help peer acceptance.

A third approach is to have regular and special education teachers team-teach a few students with autism spectrum disorder integrated into otherwise regular classes. This can be done during the whole school day or for selected portions of it. Obviously this is difficult to carry on through middle school and much easier to accomplish as partial inclusion. The special education teacher can focus on the students on the spectrum so that they continue to have helpful services that aren't usually part of inclusive placements. Stigma associated with special services may be minimized by having the students on the spectrum meet unobtrusively with the special education teacher.

Most students we see in our programs fall into the partial inclusion or fully included categories. In many cases, the school is aware of the diagnostic status of the student. However, in some cases, parents choose not to divulge the diagnosis of their child on the spectrum to school personnel. And sometimes students may go undiagnosed, with neither parent nor educator aware of the origin of the child's difficulties. Students with high-functioning autism spectrum disorders may have symptoms that are quite subtle, so that professionals who are not specifically trained to detect them often miss them. The lack of services can mean that the student is struggling academically or socially, even if symptoms are subtle.

Traditional Teacher Roles in Partially and Fully Included Classrooms

The philosophy of inclusive education calls for building a supportive school community and a strong sense of belonging in all students, which is difficult for most regular secondary school education teachers to achieve. Regular education teachers are often faced with an evaluation of their own job performance through test scores each year and have to get the most education into the most students. Middle and high school teachers have to keep track of sometimes a hundred or more students every week and have to concentrate on their academic mission. Moreover, many regular education classroom teachers and special educators are not trained to deal with the social problems presented by kids with autism spectrum disorders. Nevertheless, they face addressing the behavioral and social problems of these students. The conundrum is that if regular education teachers give students with special needs the attention they require, the teachers may not be able to meet the social and academic needs of other students. It is no surprise, then, that students with autism spectrum disorders see their teachers playing a role in providing them with support only in academic areas.

Studies show, understandably, that general education teachers tend to use strategies directed toward the class as a whole and incorporate only minor or no modifications based on student needs. On surveys, a majority of parents feel that regular education teachers do not have enough time to help their child individually. To their credit, many regular education teachers have expressed a need for additional training in facilitating the social inclusion of students with disabilities and developing strategies to reduce their loneliness and social isolation.

Research Findings on Inclusion

Research points to a mixed blessing for children with autism spectrum disorders who are placed in regular education classrooms. Such placement has been associated with increases in the complexity of their social interactions and decreases in isolative activities when compared with how they behave in special education settings.

Some parents report their child has been accepted by peers in the inclusive classroom and has even been able to form meaningful friendships with neurotypical classmates. This has been documented in a small minority of students with autism spectrum disorders. Some reports also indicate that students on the spectrum initiate more social contacts with their peers and are better able to use social skills they are taught when they are fully included. However, in many cases, it appears that inclusion alone is insufficient to truly integrate students with autism into the social networks of their neurotypical peers. Students with autism spectrum disorders typically spend a majority of their lunchtime alone or with a small social network of acquaintances, if any. Nearly half of all adolescents with autism spectrum disorders have no peer relationships at all, according to parents' reports. High-functioning students on the spectrum in inclusion settings are more often ostracized and rejected than their neurotypical classmates are.

Social Integration into School Life

Developmental psychologists have found that asking students in a classroom for their opinions on relationships with their classmates has been extremely useful in assessing the degree to which individual students fit into their peer group. One method of determining this is to ask them individually and in private how much, on a scale of 1 to 5, they would like to play with or socially interact with each other student. Then they repeat the assessment, this time asking how much they would like to work with each other student in the class. Students often rate others differently on both scales. Someone they like very much to work with may not be someone they very much like to socialize with, and vice versa. The desirable qualities of a good friend are different from the desirable qualities of someone with whom one has to work. Desirable qualities for people to work together are dependability, knowledge of the subject matter, and inclination to compromise in order to get the work done. Many students are rated highly by others as "like to work with," and improving their "like to work with" ratings is an opportunity for the teen on the spectrum to become a part of school life and certainly would be consistent with the philosophy of inclusion. Developing friendships involves other constraints that teens have to consider. These are discussed more fully in Chapter Eight.

Students with autism spectrum disorders are rated by their classmates significantly less often as being someone with whom they would like to work with and significantly more often as being someone with whom they would rather not work. We focus in this chapter and in Chapters Four through Seven, Ten, and Twelve on efforts to help teens with autism spectrum disorders fit in and be more accepted by peers as academic colleagues.

Mainstream Success of Students on the Autism Spectrum

A small minority of students with autism spectrum disorders have achieved some social and academic acceptance in inclusive settings. Studies determining the characteristics of these students point to factors these students have found helpful for themselves. These studies have identified two sets of factors that improve adjustment: the student's behavior and modifiable environmental factors.

A recent review of studies looking at differences in behaviors that influenced the acceptance of students with autism spectrum disorders in mainstream classes found that students who were most successful were those who had the highest "beneficial" traits, such as cooperation, and lowest "costly" traits, such as disruptive behavior and help seeking. Students who experienced social rejection showed the reverse pattern.

Students who were more cooperative with peers and teachers were better able to be socially accepted. This principle applied to all students, not just those on the spectrum, and probably influenced the "like to work with" ratings more than the "like to socialize with" ratings. Kids with autism spectrum disorder who were more cautiously friendly were more successful at being accepted by neurotypical peers. The implications are clear: teaching cautious social approaches may not lead to friendships, but indiscriminately trying for friendships may jeopardize "like to work with" ratings by peers and not lead to friendships anyway. Chapter Eight discusses the teacher's role in helping teens on the spectrum form friendships. The PEERS intervention program teaches cautious social approaches in the context of making friends.

Three classroom environmental factors are associated with successful inclusion of teens on the spectrum in middle and high school. First is developing a predictable and ordered environment in order to minimize these students' anxiety and help focus them better on academics. Developing schedules and ways to organize work are examples. We have listed three books for this chapter in the Resources and References section at the back of this book that are devoted to guiding parents in helping their child get organized. Second is placing the student with autism spectrum disorders in quiet, well-behaved classes. Having other students who have behavior problems or having a class run with inadequate discipline is disadvantageous not only for students on the spectrum but to all other students as well. In the next chapter, we give tips on helpful classroom management strategies. Third is providing the teen access to a knowledgeable member of the teaching or school guidance staff for advice on autism spectrum–specific issues. Students with this disorder need to learn when to ask for help, from whom, and how. It's very helpful to have someone such as a trusted guidance counselor whose door is always open and who can coach the tween and teen in problem solving. We discuss this type of support in more detail in Chapter Twelve in regard to providing a peer mentor.

We advocate a two-pronged or three-pronged approach to achieve greater acceptance for the student with autism spectrum disorder:

- Pair kids on the autism spectrum with a supervised and trained mentor (see Chapter Twelve).

- Teach these students to ask questions when they don't comprehend parts of conversations (see Chapter Six).

- Consider enlisting peers to be more tolerant when students on the autism spectrum ask them questions. This is discussed more fully in the next section. A lesson plan for this and a handout for neurotypical peers appear at the end of this chapter.

Approaches for Social Inclusion with Neurotypical Teens

In most inclusion settings, social inclusion primarily rests on the neurotypical schoolmates. The symptoms shown by teens on the spectrum are often viewed by uninformed classmates as odd, eccentric, and peculiar. Kids on the spectrum may capture the attention of their classmates by dressing as they did in elementary school, having poor hygiene and grooming, insisting the teacher follow the syllabus exactly, and being easily overwhelmed when dealing with changes or situations that are frustrating to them. They may withdraw to a quiet place when overwhelmed, which may also be noticed by peers. A typical peer reaction to these symptoms is to ignore not only the symptoms but to socially and academically ostracize the teen, who usually is sensitive to this response. He may become more anxious and perhaps have more meltdowns or withdraw even further from contact with peers.

One approach has been to encourage neurotypical students to include teens on the spectrum in their social circles. It's a mistake to ask neurotypical teens to be friends with a teen with autism spectrum disorders for three reasons. First, it is not consistent with friendship formation to ask someone to be friends for altruistic reasons. Friendship is a mutual choice, in part based on common interests. Asking neurotypical teens to befriend a teen with autism spectrum disorders because he is different would be asking them to behave unnaturally. They couldn't be genuine friends. We explore this more in Chapter Eight.

Second, telling others to be friends with a teen on the spectrum deprives them of the experience of choosing and making their own friends. It doesn't acknowledge their individual autonomy and is disabling rather than enabling. The PEERS intervention teaches teens with autism spectrum disorders how to select, make, and keep their own friends.

Third, the request to be friends with someone on the basis of a disorder may be a request that is too difficult for many neurotypical teens to comply with in earnest. Teachers are more likely to enlist students in a more whole-hearted fashion by making less demanding requests. Instead of making a broad appeal to affiliative motives, it is probably more productive to make specific appeals to altruistic motives. Instead of short-circuiting the friendship formation process, it is probably more productive to have classmates help the teen on the spectrum in small ways to better understand their peers.

Another approach is to promote greater understanding among neurotypical students about either the features of autism spectrum disorders or the specific behaviors of one of their classmates. The main thrust is usually to promote tolerance for these behaviors and cast the behaviors as not under the student's control. This approach does have some caveats. Some kids on the spectrum are undiagnosed, and both parents and teens may become upset if they are treated as a student on the spectrum. Other parents may not agree with this approach. Therefore it's usually a good idea for teachers to obtain parent and teen consent before trying this approach.

There are reports of individual parents of elementary school children who take this role on themselves. They identified their child as having autism spectrum disorder and provided educational materials and guidance for classmates as to how to handle their child's symptoms. In one case, the parents took the lead, and the teacher supported the efforts. Anecdotal reports have been that it seemed to foster tolerance of their child and, at least in the short term, proved fruitful in reducing the stress on the child.

The research evidence is not entirely supportive of disclosing and educating about diagnosis. At least in elementary school, disclosing the diagnosis of autism spectrum disorders to peers may engender more tolerance. There is also some evidence that disclosure of diagnosis and what that means will in some sense improve the behavior of peers but worsen their opinions of the child involved. For example, in one case, third and sixth graders were shown video clips of a neurotypical twelve-year-old male actor. Some showed him acting "normally." Others showed him acting "autistic." The students who saw the boy acting "autistic" rated him less favorably. When they were told that this student could not help the way he was behaving, it did not seem to change their negative opinions of the boy. Observational studies show that neurotypical children who interact with disabled children act more like parents than peers, showing physical assistance, affection, and conflict management.

Informing peers of a diagnosis and its consequences may provide neurotypical students with an alternative mode of action and thought that is somewhere between accepting and ostracism. Tolerant neurotypical students may adopt the role of helping someone less fortunate. But this can be relied on only to a limited extent and only by more altruistic teens.

Consider the example of a foreign student who has recently arrived in our country. He is unfamiliar with our customs and language and may have some customs of his own that we may find peculiar. Simply tolerating him would be doing him a disservice. Most of us would try to help him become familiar with our culture in small ways without adopting a "guide" role.

We propose enlisting a segment of kids who are more altruistic to help students on the autism spectrum in similar small ways. Since we are proposing a strategy that is not asking for much personal involvement, these tweens and teens might in the aggregate make a positive and sustained impact on the student on the spectrum.

Teen Altruism

Recent studies of altruism in teens show that altruism increases with age. Perhaps it is teachers and community leaders who are able to change teens from more egocentric to more altruistic adults. As you probably would expect, altruistic behavior is more common in teen girls than teen boys. Comparisons of teacher reports and child reports indicate that teachers are not particularly good at judging who has the most altruistic motives. Interestingly, the most truly altruistic teens (those who would demonstrate kindness when anonymous) are those who are not strongly influenced by public approval. The message here is not to write off any students as having potential for altruistic behavior. And there are many teens who are altruistic primarily when they are being observed. It is important to enlist these teens also and provide some public acknowledgment for their deeds, even if not truly genuine, in order to make a change in the peer culture.

We present Lesson Plan 2.1 for instructing neurotypical students on features of autism spectrum disorders and how best to help, along with Handout 2.1. A thoughtful brochure on the Autism Society of America Web site has a similar purpose, and we have borrowed some of the points from it (see Useful Resources for this chapter in the Resources and References section). The materials and lesson plan that follow can be used to enlist an altruistic segment of students or a single cross-age peer mentor (see Chapter Twelve) or both.

LESSON PLAN 2.1 Helping Students with Autism Spectrum Disorder

Social Skills Success for Students with Autism/Asperger's, copyright © 2011 John Wiley and Sons, Inc.

SELECTED STUDENT NEED

- Enlisting neurotypical students to help students with autism spectrum disorders learn social rules

LEARNING OBJECTIVES

- Students will learn about the strengths and challenges of students with autism spectrum disorder.
- Students will learn how to help students with autism spectrum disorder learn the social rules.

STANDARD AND BENCHMARK

- Observe more positive interaction between neurotypical students and students with autism spectrum disorder.

MATERIAL AND RESOURCE

- Handout 2.1: "What Is Autism Spectrum Disorder?"

Introduction

The purpose of this class is to have neurotypical students reexamine their opinions of teens with autism spectrum disorders and be more willing to offer to help them learn better social graces.

The Class Session

1. Start with, "Today we are going to learn a little about what it's like to have a disability called autism spectrum disorder. I want you to turn to the person sitting next to you. Both of you close your eyes while taking turns talking. Either talk about something nice that happened to you or something irritating that happened in the last couple of days. During this conversation I want you to consciously **not** change your voice tone while you are talking. Speak in a monotone. Also try to slow down your speech."

2. Limit this activity to no more than about five minutes total. After about two minutes, have the students switch speaker and listener roles.

3. At the end of the exercise, have students report how they felt in both talking and listening roles without having cues from the other person's body language and voice tone. Have them identify what parts of their conversation depend more on these cues—for example, sarcasm, irony, some slang words, and communicating emotions.

4. Say to the class, "The exercise you just participated in was meant to give you a bit of an idea of what it must be like for someone with autism spectrum disorders. The difference is that you have had experience throughout your life of learning how to read the body language and voice tones of others. Kids with autism spectrum may have missed that learning through much of their lives."

5. Pass out Handout 2.1, and read the first paragraph.

6. Ask the students as a group (with the caution to not divulge any names) to raise their hands if they know anyone with autism spectrum disorders. Then figure out together how many students at your school have autism spectrum disorder (the usual rate is about 1 in 150, or 10 students in a student body of 1,500). Announce about how many students at your school have autism spectrum disorder based on this calculation.

7. Have individual students take turns reading each bullet point in the handout. Have students think of more examples of each if they can.

8. You might point out a Web site students can look at, like that of the Autism Society of America: http://www.autism-society.org/. Or they can see or rent movies about the lives of people with autism spectrum disorder, for instance, *Temple Grandin.* You can ask if anyone has seen a movie on people with autism spectrum disorder. The movie *Rain Man* (1988), for example, is about a man with severe disabilities due to autism spectrum disorder. Relatively few people with the disorder have disabilities as severe as the main character.

Homework Assignment

None

Assessment

Make note of the additional ways that students have come up with to understand autism spectrum disorder as a disability.

Social Skills Success for Students with Autism/Asperger's, copyright © 2011 John Wiley and Sons, Inc.

HANDOUT 2.1 What Is Autism Spectrum Disorder?

There are some kids among us who have problems communicating and understanding others. They also may have some behaviors that we think are unusual. If you take the time, you will see that they want to be a part of school life but don't understand a lot about it and don't know how to fit in. The students we are talking about have what's called *autism spectrum disorder.*

When they were younger, many of them were isolated from others. As they grew up, they overcame a lot of barriers they faced and are now trying to understand others. But they have fallen behind in this understanding by being isolated for so long.

Here are some facts about autism spectrum disorder:

- Autism spectrum disorder is a disorder that we don't fully understand that involves parts of the brain. It is not a disease and is not contagious, but there is no cure.
- As many as 1 in 150 people are thought to have autism spectrum disorder.
- It's about seven times more common in boys than girls.
- Teens with autism spectrum disorder want to fit in and usually don't choose to act differently from other teens.
- They act differently because they may not be aware that their behavior looks unusual to others.
- Teens with autism spectrum disorder are as different from each other as you and I are.

Here are some strengths they may have:

- Some can be experts about certain things like computers, video games, science, or baseball statistics.
- Some are very good at memorizing.
- Some are very good at noticing small details.
- Most are not defensive about being helped and often are eager to learn.
- They rarely tell a lie.

Here are some challenges that they may have and what you can do to help:

DIFFICULTY WITH ORDINARY CONVERSATION

- They may forget to use greetings and closings, such as "hello" and "good-bye." And they may not understand that when they are asked, "How are you?" they don't need to give a long answer. Cut them some slack. You might even say after asking them "How are you?" that it requires only a one- or two-word answer like "Okay."

- They may not understand slang (such as "get over it," "let's hang out," "put a sock in it," or "take a chill pill").

- They may not understand jokes or sarcasm and forget to ask when they don't understand. If they ask, please be patient and explain the joke. They want to learn.

- Sometimes they don't understand what you are telling them. Help them to feel comfortable asking questions when they don't understand.

- They may have anxiety attacks, especially when they are under pressure. You may not be able to tell that they are anxious at first. They may need help finding a secluded place to "chill out."

- They may not understand vague requests, such as "Come back later." It is better to be specific, for example, "Come back in fifteen minutes."

DIFFICULTY WITH BODY LANGUAGE

- They may either stand too close or too far away in conversation. Tell them you are more comfortable if they stand at arm's distance from you.

- They may not understand hints. Please tell them directly.

DIFFICULTY UNDERSTANDING COMMON SOCIAL SITUATIONS

- They may not have learned common sense about things you take for granted. For instance, they may not have enough common sense to avoid telling others when they break minor school rules.

- They may make unintentionally rude comments, such as "You have bad breath."

- They may benefit from gentle guidance about grooming and hygiene. You can pick one thing (spitting when talking) and tell them briefly how they can change (in a warm voice, "Say it, don't spray it!").

STUCK FOLLOWING ROUTINES AND RULES

- They may get stuck in following rules.

- They are strongly tied to routines. They benefit greatly when being told in detail and in advance of impending changes.

- See if, with gentle feedback from you, they will learn from their mistakes.

Many kids with autism spectrum disorder work hard to learn appropriate behaviors and how to interpret emotional meaning. With your help, they can continue to learn about themselves and their classmates. Remember that a student with autism spectrum disorder is really just another adolescent who wants to be respected as an individual and have fun.

CHAPTER 3

Classroom Management and Social Skills Groups

> *Parents of teens with Asperger Syndrome face many problems that other parents do not. Time is running out for teaching their Aspie how to become an independent adult. As one mother put it, 'There's so little time, and so much left to do.' ... Meanwhile, their immature Aspie is often indifferent or even hostile to these concerns .... Like all teenagers, he is harder to control and less likely to listen to his parents. He may be tired of parents nagging him to ... brush his teeth, and wake up in time for school. He may hate school because he is dealing with social ostracism or academic failure there.*

—From "The Asperger's Teen," in *Your Little Professor*
(http://www.yourlittleprofessor.com/teen2.html)

This chapter first reviews techniques to improve the classroom management of kids on the spectrum. Many teachers, especially those in the field of special education, have been trained to use classroom management techniques or have discovered them through trial and error. We review what we have found to be most effective for conducting a social skills lesson or for use in classrooms with at least one student on the spectrum. This chapter then reviews our tips for holding social skills groups on school campuses.

We look at how to involve parents in the interventions. The lesson plans in this book focus on how teachers can make an impact in integrating teens on the spectrum into school life. Some of these lesson plans incorporate contact with parents. The hope is that they will recognize changes in their teen's social competence and will support these at home. Some teachers may wish to meet directly with parents to solidify this alliance, and some will want to conduct social skills groups like the ones detailed in the PEERS manual, *Skills for Teenagers with Developmental and Autism Spectrum Disorders: The PEERS Treatment Manual.* This chapter therefore provides some tips as to how to begin these meetings.

Classroom Management for Students with Autism Spectrum Disorders

The level of inclusion dictates the types of classroom management techniques that are most practical for teachers to use. Segregated classrooms with only a few kids and a high student-to-teacher ratio means that teachers can use more intensive management techniques. Fully included classrooms require less intensive interventions because the students have more skills to begin with (or else they are not in the correct educational environment). This chapter is meant only to highlight important concepts rather than to present comprehensive management programs. The Resources and References section of this book lists more comprehensive sources for classroom management techniques and programs.

Segregated Students

Behavioral approaches have been successful in modifying problem behaviors for children and teens with autism spectrum disorders. Three features are necessary for these programs to be successful:

1. Define individual target behaviors in specific and observable terms—for example, "Stays in seat with no more than one reminder every thirty minutes."

2. Deliver praise and reward frequently; for instance, give one point every thirty minutes for a student who remains seated.

3. Offer a longer-term reward to motivate more frequent compliance. For example, for accumulating a certain number of points over a specific period, a student gets a special reward—say, listening to music while working, eating lunch outside on a nice day, talk time at the end of class, or rewards that signify appreciation, such as bookmarks, erasers, pencils and pens, and even books. Rewards should consume minimal or no valuable instruction time.

This reward system has two important modifications over those typically used in middle school classrooms. First, rewards should not involve associating with friends, because kids without friends in the class would be singled out. Second, reward programs should not be applied to the class as a whole. The student with autism spectrum disorders would be stigmatized if he were the one responsible for the whole class losing a reward. Poor behavior is better addressed with individual consequences, such as just the student in question not getting the end-of-week reward.

Partially Included Students

Since partially included students are often in a transition phase, any anxieties they have are likely to be heightened. The general principle to apply here is to make the new environment as easy to cope with as possible, especially at first. It is especially important for these students' transition into fully included classrooms that other students in the transition classroom have only minimal or no behavioral problems. Continuing behavioral disruption heightens everyone's anxiety (students and teachers alike). This classroom anxiety will add to the anxieties of the student on the spectrum. Greater anxiety will impair functioning at a time when the student on the spectrum should be making the best first impression possible.

It is also important to consider the changes in classroom structure for teens on the spectrum in a transition phase. If the segregated classroom had lots of behavioral interventions, then it will be a sudden shock for a teen on the spectrum to go into a minimally managed classroom. He will expect lots of monitoring and rewards and may be puzzled as to why these supports are lacking in his new classroom. Adequate preparation about the differences between classrooms may be an important factor in ensuring a smooth transition.

Fully Included Students

The behavioral approaches reviewed for segregated classrooms, which typically have no more than ten students, are impractical for inclusive middle school and high school settings where teachers typically have twenty or more students in a class. Attempting to implement programs individualized for a specific adolescent with autism spectrum disorders would mean neglecting the rest of the class.

The following strategies, helpful for the kid on the spectrum, are readily employed in larger classrooms. It is especially helpful to implement these classroom strategies immediately at the beginning of the school year in order to set the tone:

1. Arrange furniture in your classroom so that you can easily move around and stand near any student you want. Moving around as you talk is more engaging for students than staying in one place at the head of the class. This way no student can hide in the back and become disengaged.

2. Have specific, well-described routines for students to follow when they come into class, sit down, and take out their materials. The same routine at the beginning of each class is very helpful for teens on the spectrum and neurotypical teens too.

3. Post no more than five simple classroom rules prominently in front of the class for all to see. The rules should be consistently enforced all of the time. The rules should be stated as behaviors you want students to follow and in language that is easily observable—for example, "Remain in your seat at all times with your eyes facing front." Avoid rules such as, "Don't get out of your seat." Positive rules set a positive tone for the class. Teens on the spectrum love rules, and neurotypical teens are usually grateful for clear guidelines too. Here are some rules one teacher found to be effective in covering most classroom behavior:

   - Stay in your seat unless you get permission from the teacher to leave.

   - Raise your hand to speak.

- You may ask for a hallway pass 10 minutes after the start and up to 10 minutes before the end of class.

- Keep your hands, feet, and all objects to yourself.

4. Use a signal to quiet the class at the beginning of instruction. Two fingers up in the shape of a "V" is a good one. This is a great way to avoid yelling over the buzz of students as they come into a classroom, and it shows that you are in charge.

5. Make seat assignments so that students who need extra attention from you will be closer to where you spend most of your time. Make these assignments to all students in the class so as not to single out students needing the special seating and to avoid placing potentially talkative friends together.

Consequences for Misbehavior

Occasionally it may be necessary to give negative consequences for disruptive behavior for some teens on the spectrum. These consequences should increase in severity with continued misbehavior. For instance, the teacher walks up to within two feet of a teen who is being disruptive and says, "Please sit quietly and listen." He or she then waits next to the student until the student begins to comply or goes on to the next step to show that the teacher means business.

Notice that this command is worded as a behavior that the teen needs to start doing rather than as a behavior he needs to stop. Positive statements help kids focus on what they should be doing and maintain a positive tone in the classroom. A prime example of the effects of negatively worded commands is to ask someone, "Don't think of an elephant." This always results in starting to think about the forbidden object.

Also notice that in this intervention, the teacher is speaking directly to the disruptive student rather than to the class as a whole. This avoids inadvertently punishing well-behaved students, which would be confusing for a student on the spectrum who is behaving well. In addition, group reprimands and consequences place additional stigma on the student on the spectrum if he happens to be the one misbehaving; moreover, he may not understand that he is the target.

Some teachers use nonverbal messages, such as quietly standing next to a student or clearing his or her throat, thereby giving a nonverbal message to stop an ongoing behavior. This may be too subtle for adolescents with autism spectrum disorders because they have trouble interpreting body language.

If the teen continues to disrupt the session, he gets a warning of a specific impending consequence, for example, "Please sit quietly and listen or you will lose your point for the half-hour," or, "Eyes front and quiet please, or you will sit with me for the first five minutes of recess." Students should get only one warning before the consequence is delivered. If they get more than one warning before the consequence is applied, the warnings lose their effectiveness.

Warning before an impending consequence gives the student a chance to stop the misbehavior before you have to take action. Warnings that are effectively backed up with consequences save time and save the use of negative consequences for only the most severe situations, since the warning alone comes to be enough to stop misbehavior.

Short consequences are better than longer ones. Loss of five minutes of recess allows for multiple consequences, so if recess is twenty minutes, for example, you have four available consequences you can give, which will have a huge impact on recess.

For continued rule violations, the next level up might be a phone call home to parents informing them of chronic misbehavior. It is always beneficial to warn the teen that this is about to happen in order to provide an opportunity for him to stop misbehaving before you have to deliver this consequence. The final level up and the one initially used for more severe behavior is an immediate referral to the principal's office.

Organizing Social Skills Groups for Tweens and Teens

Teachers who conduct social skills classes have many advantages over therapists who are running groups in the community. The student–teacher relationship has always been unique and special. The teacher is often a trusted adult and experiences little conflict with the teen (especially if he or she uses effective class management techniques), in sharp contrast to the experiences of the teen's parents and siblings. This is no less true for the relationship between the student with autism spectrum disorders and his teachers. Most important, teachers have access to the teen's peer group that is unrivaled among professionals doing social skills training. Thus, teachers are in many ways the ideal professional to run social skills groups for teens on the spectrum. Getting a social skills group going is no easy matter, unless it is a regular part of the school curriculum.

How to Organize Groups at School

Students on the spectrum are sensitive to the stigma of needing a social skills group. The best time to run a social skills class for kids with autism spectrum disorders who are fully included is after school. If you are planning a concurrent parent group, then after regular working hours for both groups is best. Ideally, the class should be located in some out-of-the-way part of the school so that others do not pass by.

Higher-functioning teens on the spectrum are sensitive to the range of social functioning of other teens in such a group. Too wide a range in functioning may be taken as an indication that the higher-functioning teens are lower functioning than they actually are. Carefully screen a potential group for social functioning. Keep in mind that overall academic ability is not a good measure of this. Verbal ability is a better measure but still not good enough to use for this screening. The best way to establish social functioning is to evaluate recreational interests: games the students can and like to play, movies and TV they are interested in watching, topics they like to talk about. Students with narrow interests make this assessment more difficult. Chapter Four discusses how to expand these interests, which is probably a good idea to do before starting such groups. Additional screening guidelines and interview formats are provided in the beginning of the PEERS manual.

How to Have Teens Take the Class

Introducing the idea of a social skills group in terms of activities is the best way to broach it with kids. We tell them, "We have a class that teaches how to make and keep friends. Is that something you might be interested in?" Avoid trying to sell them on the group as something they need (although teens on the spectrum are more likely to admit they need this group than other teens who require social skills training).

How to Engage Teens in Class Discussions

The Socratic approach to teaching the material is often helpful to teens on the spectrum. Often you can start by modeling a scene using examples with strikingly wrong behavior and have them point out what's incorrect. Because kids on the spectrum love to point out things that are wrong or incorrect, this approach involves them in the process and also frames the lesson, pinpointing the "wrong" item for them to inspect more carefully. After this, you can repeat the same scene and model how it is done competently. Have them point out what is correct, and they will be focused on the parts of the scene of most instructive value.

Have Some Fun Activities

If you are not conducting social skills classes during regular school hours as part of the regular curriculum, enrollment and attendance can become problems. Including a fun interactive activity after each lesson will resolve this problem. Examples are board games or informal sports activities. The PEERS manual describes tried-and-true activities for each of the fourteen lessons. These activities are closely related to skills that the teens need to acquire during each lesson.

Have "Real-Life" Homework

Homework assignments are essential for generalization to occur. The PEERS program uses parent-supervised phone calls from home to practice conversational skills and parent-supervised get-togethers with other teens to practice social skills with peers. The following features ensure that students will do the assignment:

1. Assign a date and time and other participant to the assignment. For example, the PEERS program has parents and teens agree on whom the teen will call on the phone to practice conversational skills.

2. Make the assignments easy at first, and gradually have them become more difficult.

3. Discuss the potential barriers the teen might have to overcome in order to attempt the homework and how to get around these barriers.

4. Debrief teens on the previous homework assignment as the first item on the agenda for the next class.

Involving Parents in Social Skills Training

There are two main options for involving parents. The first is to have weekly group sessions where parents review what has been done with their child. The teacher can go over any letters or handouts and gather any assessments necessary. This is clearly the better option in terms of ensuring that the teen practices skills at places other than school, including at home. Most parents want and like to be engaged as allies in programs for their teen on the spectrum. Weekly sessions, such as those described in the PEERS manual, will keep everyone engaged.

The disadvantages to this option are that parents who are unable to participate due to economic or geographical circumstances are left out. It also requires an extra time commitment on the part of the teacher to meet with parents at times the parents are available. If the parent groups do not meet during school hours, parents must arrange child care, which may limit the participation of poorer families. Having both the teen and parent sessions at the same time avoids stigma but requires two teachers instead of one.

The second option is to maintain communication with the parent by sending letters and other material to their home but not having a formal parent session. The teacher should be available to answer any questions the parent might have about the material. This will keep parents involved, although not to the level of the first option. This is the approach used in the lesson plans of this book.

All of the lesson plans in this book are designed for the second option, although the lesson for expanding interests in Chapter Four is more effective when the teacher can meet with parents as a group. In addition, we strongly advise teachers to get parental consent before proceeding with the modules on teaching acceptance of teens with autism spectrum disorders (Chapter Two), handling anxiety and meltdowns (Chapter Ten), and training peer mentors (Chapter Twelve).

PART TWO

INTERVENTIONS FOR BASIC SOCIAL SKILLS

CHAPTER 4

Helping Students Expand Their Interests

> *Arthur memorized all the NBA statistics better than any commissioner. He was trying to be a jock. Although he was on the basketball team, he was never allowed to play during a game because he was quite awkward. In addition, he didn't pass to teammates once he had the ball, and his shots were inaccurate.*

Kids on the spectrum are noted for their often restricted range of interests. Some delight in talking about an interest that may be age appropriate, but persist to the point where the details wear on the listener. Others talk at great length about topics so esoteric as to be of little interest to most others of the same age. This is more evident in teens on the spectrum who are lower functioning or younger, but it can apply to high-functioning teens as well.

Problems in Conversation Versus Problems in Interests

One approach to addressing this problem is to focus on this apparent conversational deficit by attempting to teach better conversational skills. The idea is to teach these adolescents how to share a conversation and listen to others better. However, research has shown that students on the spectrum may have restricted interests without significant social communication difficulties and vice versa. A more fruitful approach may be to view this as a deficit in the breadth of their interests. Perhaps they have nothing else to talk about and can't relate to what others want to talk about because they have not experienced it themselves. The idea is to give them more to talk about, and eventually their conversations will improve. Interviews with adults on the spectrum have shown that most had restricted interests as children but were willing to expand their interests in order to fit in better to their social environment. By reducing the time they spent on their restricted interest (sometimes by making a schedule to limit this), they could expand their interests to become more realistic. In most cases, parents were central to this expansion.

A twelve-year-old on the spectrum whom we met liked only to watch daytime soap operas on TV and spent all of her leisure time in front of the TV. The activity kept her away from peers. Moreover, her narrow interest generated conversation only pertaining to daytime soap opera plots and characters, a topic of little interest to her peers. When the other kids wanted to talk about going to the mall, she had not been there enough to know what they were talking about. Her peers came to expect that all she wanted to talk about was the soaps and started to avoid her for fear of getting trapped in this narrow conversation.

Aside from conversational problems, narrow interests confined her source of peers to her school classmates. This is a problem for many teens on the spectrum. The few teens they know are exclusively at school. The feeling of fitting in is stronger when they see their schoolmates in different contexts. A wider range of interests allows teens on the spectrum to meet people who are more like them in terms of these common interests. Therefore, it is imperative to widen the interest range of teens on the spectrum.

Socially Functional Interests

Mutual interests are the basis of friendships. They are the excuse for getting together and getting to know each other better. Kids tend to associate with those who have similar interests. They start to coalesce into crowds (for example, computer geeks and jocks) and send each other signals with dress, musical tastes, and the slang terms they use in conversation identifying the crowd to which they belong. They feel more comfortable and better supported when they have interests that help them fit into a crowd. Kids lacking sufficient interests will have fewer meaningful conversations with their peers and fewer continuing interactions, and they will lack direction as to which crowd they should approach for more comfortable interactions.

Only interests and associated activities with interactive features will be useful. When choosing to explore a new interest with a tween or teen, consider how the potential interest fits the following criteria for interests and related activities:

- The potential activity should involve talking with other teens about the shared interest—for example, a video game club where teens talk about their games. One in which kids just play the games and then go home is not socially useful.

- A potential interest should have wide enough appeal to attract many others. This will enlarge the pool of potential friends and help the teen fit in better at school.

- Activities related to the interest should take place after school in the teen's neighborhood or within a short walk, bike ride, or drive. Not only will the activity itself be easy to get to, but it will more likely involve other kids who live nearby and can continue to get together as the relationship develops.

- The potential activity should involve something that can be done weekly—for example, a chess club that meets once a week to discuss and play chess. Activities such as hiking or camping are done only rarely so will not promote enough peer contact to develop friendships.

Interference Due to Anxiety

It is also important to assess anxiety levels in adolescents on the spectrum to see if anxiety is preventing a tween or teen from branching out. Fifty to 75 percent of teens on the spectrum have anxiety disorders that can interfere with their motivation to seek new interests. Sometimes it is unclear whether anxiety has prevented the teen from branching out in the past or whether it is competing with the teen's motivation to find new interests now. Review Chapter Nine to determine if a student has an anxiety disorder before turning to the lesson plans in this chapter. If signs are present for any anxiety disorder, then proceed to Chapter Ten. After teaching the teen to cope with his anxiety, then proceed with the lesson plans in this chapter.

Building on Current Interests

An easier way to expand a teen's interests might be to build on interests the teen already has. Some seemingly solitary interests may be expanded to be socially useful. For instance, a teen interested in video games and computers can talk about them with his peers. These interests are common among all teenage boys as well as teenage boys on the spectrum. The next step is to find activities that involve talking about video and computer games rather than just quietly playing them alone. Boys can trade secrets about how to get to the next level of the game and inform each other as to new or related games. The bottom line is that interests dictate leisure-time activities, and the reverse is also true: getting a teen to try new activities may stimulate interest. Leisure-time activities are a great way for young people to make more acquaintances and boost their reputation among peers, both inside and outside school. The motivation for adolescents to explore interests is that many of them want to be a part of school life and don't know how. Lesson Plan 4.1 has teens listen to each other's experiences with leisure-time interests in order to motivate them to try a new interest. This also may give them enough information about a particular new interest to decrease any anxieties they have about trying it themselves.

Assessing Student Interests

High-functioning students on the spectrum differ considerably from each other in how restricted their interests are, as well as the nature of their interests. While some may have a wide variety, the activities may be more appropriate for younger children. Because of large differences in individuals, it is helpful for teachers to explore students' breadth of interest before beginning Lesson 4.1. They can assess how socially useful each teen's interest is to help them fit in with peers by having the teens complete the interest survey in Handout 4.1. Giving a list of interests, as in the interest survey, may be helpful for assessment and for helping to tailor a more rewarding classroom experience. Teachers may also add school-based or local activities they know about in the blank boxes of the first part of this survey before handing it out. Students can use the blank spaces at the bottom if they have any interests not listed in the boxes. The lesson instructor may become an expert on interests available in the area as he or she has successive years of addressing peer relationships.

HANDOUT 4.1 Student Interest Survey

Read each activity below, and put a check mark next to each you are interested in trying (the Interest column) or already do this activity (the Doing column). If you are doing this activity and like it, put a star next to it.

ACTIVITY	INTEREST	DOING	ACTIVITY	INTEREST	DOING
Acting			Costume role play		
Amateur/ham radio			Crafts (for example, woodworking, needlepoint)		
Animals/pets			Dancing/drill team		
Art			Darts		
Astronomy			Electronics		
Baseball			Embroidery		
Basketball			Fishing		
Beachcombing			Football		
Bicycling (for example, mountain, BMX)			Golf		
Board games			Horseback riding		
Body building			Internet activities		
Bowling			Magic		
Camping/hiking			Making models (for example, cars)		
Cards			Metal detecting		
Chess			Movies		
Church			Music—instruments/ playing in a band		
Computer activities			Music—listening		
Cooking			Music—concerts		

Social Skills Success for Students with Autism/Asperger's, copyright © 2011 John Wiley and Sons, Inc.

ACTIVITY	INTEREST	DOING	ACTIVITY	INTEREST	DOING
Paintball			Sketching		
Photography			Star Trek		
Playing team sports			Teen magazines		
Radio-controlled boats, cars, and other vehicles			Video games		
Singing in choir, chorus, or a band			Watching sporting events		
Skateboarding					

Please list any other interests you may have that you can share with others:

_____   _____   _____

_____   _____   _____

_____   _____   _____

_____   _____   _____

_____   _____   _____

Source: Adapted from Not so boring life.com: http://www.notsoboringlife.com/list-of-hobbies/.

After the students complete the form in class, collect them. Send a blank form home with students along with the cover letter provided as the parent interest survey letter in Handout 4.2. It is often helpful to have the teen's parent fill out the interest survey form too because parents sometimes have a different view of the teen's potential and actual interests. You want to see if parents can add more possibilities to the potential interest list. Ask parents to complete the form without sharing their responses with their teen. Have parents return the completed forms well before using Lesson Plan 4.1 to allow you enough time to look at them and compare them with the teen-completed surveys. If there is nothing checked in the "Doing" columns, the teen has an interest deficit. Either the teen or the parent might have checked old or new interests the teen might try in the "Interest" columns.

Lessons to Expand Interests

Lesson Plans 4.1 and 4.2 divide the instruction into thinking about a new activity for the teen to try and actually trying it. Handout 4.1 and class instruction motivate the teen to first pick an activity that he or she probably will like (Lesson Plan 4.1) and try out the homework with parent help (Lesson Plan 4.2 and Handout 4.3). The next step is to contract with the individual kids with interest deficits to try a new interest. Although the materials are provided to promote parent participation by themselves, you may want to have more extensive parent contact in case they have problems or questions about their roles in the assignments. Encouraging parents to call you with questions after each lesson is a good practice.

You may have to meet privately with students who have difficulty doing the homework.

HANDOUT 4.2 Parent Interest Survey Letter

Dear Parent,

Over the next few weeks we will be working on assessing and developing leisure-time activity interests for your child. We know that many students with autism spectrum disorders have restricted interests that often are not useful in helping them fit in better at school. In contrast, we find that some interests will attract potential friends.

I am enclosing a blank Student Interest Survey. We have had your child complete one in class. Please complete the survey without discussing your answers with your child, so that we can have your independent assessment of your child's interests.

When you fill out the form:

- Indicate with a check mark those activities your child currently does at least twice per month in the "Doing" columns.
- Indicate with a star (*) the activities you've noticed your child enjoys.
- Indicate with a check mark the activities your child might be willing to try in the "Interest" columns.

Feel free to suggest other activities I haven't listed in the blank spaces at the end of the form.

Please complete this interest survey, and return it to me by _____.

Thank you for your help with this assessment.

Sincerely,

LESSON PLAN 4.1 Exploring New Interests

SELECTED STUDENT NEED

- Expanding interests to attract and meet potential friends.

LEARNING OBJECTIVES

- Students with restricted interests will be able to add at least one new interest that may lead to meeting new friends.
- Students will identify activities that have not led to friendships.

STANDARDS AND BENCHMARKS

- Select one or two new interests that the student wishes to try with parent.
- Become accurate in selecting new interests.

MATERIALS AND RESOURCES

- Handout 4.1, "Student Interest Survey," completed by each teen and his parent prior to the beginning of the lesson. Review these surveys to divide teens into those who need help to expand their interests and those who have interests they can present in class.
- Handout 4.3, "Getting Your Child to Expand Interests to Fit In with Peers," is an aid for parents to help their teen complete the homework assigned at the end of the lesson.

Introduction

The purpose of this class is to motivate students with restricted interests to think of new activities they would like to try.

The Class Session

Start with this introduction:

Today we are going to explore the activities we do for fun that we do with others. Most teens have activities they do for fun. Sometimes we see them having fun at lunch, and sometimes they are having fun, but we don't see them while they are having fun, like when they are meeting with their clubs after school or outside school. I have had each of you fill out a form listing the activities you might do or want to do. Right now I would like to hear from students who have indicated activities they like that they already do on a regular basis. I would like each of you to tell me [write these on the board as you are presenting them] (1) if you had fun (if not, pick another activity), (2) what you do at the activity, (3) whether anyone else does the activity with you and you know that person from

LESSON PLAN 4.1 (continued)

someplace other than school, and (4) what you did at the last meeting. Tell us as many details as you would like to share about this meeting. I will give you each about five minutes to talk.

I'll start first with an activity that I like to do.

Then present this activity, using the format you just outlined, for about five minutes.

Next, call on a teen who indicated on his survey that he had such an activity and who will best be able to talk about this. Ask the questions, just as if you were having a conversation with him, about the activity. Unless you need to ask him to speak loud enough to be heard, focus only on the answers to the questions you pose. Get as many details about the activities as possible. This may help desensitize the more anxious teens who need to expand their activities.

Encourage the rest of the class to ask positive questions about the activity to help the teen present his interest in as good a light as possible. Then continue having teens present their interests and ask if anyone has tried a new interest that he or she would like to talk about.

This first session will set the stage and motivate teens with limited interests to expand them. Allow one or two weeks before the lesson outlined in Lesson Plan 4.2 to give parents and teens enough time for the homework assignment.

Homework Assignment

Teens are to review Handout 4.3 with their parent and select one or two new activities they would like to try.

Assessment

Make note of the interests the teens are developing as they hear about the activities presented by others. Repeat this lesson until all of the teens who already have extracurricular activities can talk about them. Begin the lesson set out in Lesson Plan 4.2 after about one or two weeks and there are still students who want to talk about activities they are already doing.

HANDOUT 4.3 Getting Your Child to Expand Interests to Fit In with Peers

Your child can benefit greatly from expanding his or her leisure-time interests. Some interests help a teen to fit in better with others. When teens have interests in common, their conversation flows more easily and they know which crowd they belong with. The following activities help teens fit in:

1. The activity should involve **talking** with other kids who share the interest. A video game club, where teens talk about their games, is more beneficial than one in which teens just play the games and then go home.

2. The activity should **have wide enough appeal** to attract many others who are at the same social maturity level as your child.

3. Activities should **take place in your neighborhood after school** or a short distance away so that your child can do them regularly.

4. The activity should **take place on a weekly basis.** Clubs that meet weekly have plenty to talk about. Activities that are done sporadically, such as hiking or camping, may not have enough regular involvement, so getting your child to go to these may be more of a problem.

5. The activity should have adequate adult supervision.

We have made **selecting** a new activity a homework assignment, so that teens will be more motivated to comply. The teen will report his choices for new activities in class. **Now is your best chance to get your child to pick a new activity to expand his or her interests.**

Before talking to your child about selecting a new activity:

- *Pick activities likely to be successful.* Ideas for these should come from the Student Interest Survey that you and your child completed, from after-school activities, or from your child's past activities. Think again about activities that your child has tried in the past and still hold interest.

- *Investigate the possible activity.* Before discussing a new activity with your child, call the adult in charge. Describe how competent your child is at the activity and any other characteristic that you think might affect his or her participation. Keep in mind that it is not important to be among the best at the activity, but to be at a level of competence similar to the others who participate. Ask for the names of other kids who also participate (maybe your child already knows them), and find out the time and frequency of meetings. Decide if it will work with your schedule and if the adult supervisor seems easy to work with.

Talk to your child about the activity. Once you have the details of one or two promising activities, briefly present them to your child as opportunities to complete his or her class homework assignment. **Your child is not to try out a new activity yet, only select one or two to try later.**

Social Skills Success for Students with Autism/Asperger's, copyright © 2011 John Wiley and Sons, Inc.

LESSON PLAN 4.2 Trying New Interests

SELECTED STUDENT NEED

- Expanding interests to attract and meet new peers.

LEARNING OBJECTIVE

- Students with restricted interests will be able to add at least one new interest that may lead to meeting new peers.

STANDARDS AND BENCHMARKS

- Attend a meeting for a new activity; the parent may be present.
- Become accurate in selecting new interests.

MATERIAL AND RESOURCE

- Handout 4.4 for parents: "Getting Your Child to Try New Activities to Fit In with Peers."

Introduction

The purpose of this class is to motivate teens with restricted interests to try new activities through fulfilling a homework assignment.

The Class Session

Introduce the class in this way:

> Today we are going to continue with our reports of activities that some of you have been attending. We would also like the rest of you to find some new activities to try, so that you can report on your new activity over the next weeks. I will continue to ask you if (1) you had fun (if not, pick another activity), (2) what you do at the activity, (3) whether there was someone who does the activity with you whom you know from someplace else, and (4) what you did at the last meeting.

> Tell us as many details as you would like to share about this meeting. I will give you each about five minutes to talk.

Encourage the rest of the class to ask positive questions about the activity, to help the teen present his interest in as good a light as possible.

Continue to get details from each teen. Go over the parent handout (Handout 4.4) with the teens and answer any questions the teens have. The homework is optional for teens who already have sufficient activities. For each teen needing to report (one who is trying a new interest), ask what he decided with his

LESSON PLAN 4.2   (continued)

parents was going to be his activity. Praise good choices that fit the following criteria (from Handout 4.3):

1. The activity should involve **talking** with other teens who share the interest. A video game club, where teens talk about their games, is more beneficial than one in which teens just play the games and then go home.

2. The activity should **have wide enough appeal** to attract many others who are at the same social maturity level as the teen.

3. Activities should **take place in the teen's neighborhood** or within a short distance, so that the teen can do them more often.

4. The activity should **take place on a weekly basis.** Clubs that meet weekly have plenty to talk about. Activities that are done sporadically, such as hiking or camping, may not have enough regular involvement, so getting the teen to continue to go to these may be more of a problem.

5. The activity should have adequate adult supervision.

Homework Assignment

Teens are to review Handout 4.4 with their parent and try the new activity they selected. This homework is optional for teens who have sufficient interests.

Assessment

Make note of the interests the students are developing as they hear activities presented by others.

Social Skills Success for Students with Autism/Asperger's, copyright © 2011 John Wiley and Sons, Inc.

HANDOUT 4.4 Getting Your Child to Try New Activities to Fit In with Peers

This week your child is to try out the new activity he or she has selected. Some kids are interested in trying out new activities. Others may seem uninterested in trying new things, but it may be that they are actually anxious. You can use the steps below to make it easier for your child to give a new activity a chance. Make it clear that your child is not promising to join for a long time, only to give it a try (this will help his or her anxiety about trying new things).

STEPS TO GETTING YOUR CHILD TO TRY A NEW ACTIVITY

1. Decide with your child how he or she will try it out

   - *Without you there.* Some teens may be embarrassed to be with parents, so the parent might not be present. In this case, ensure that your child gets to the activity on time and pick him up after it is over.

   - *With you in the background.* You ensure that your child gets to the activity on time and then fade into the background, sitting in the back of the activity and watch how he participates. Allow him to participate at his own pace.

   - *Sitting together with you in the background.* Both of you watch the activity. When your child gets more comfortable, you can fade into the background.

2. Make a deal with your child to observe, if your child resists going: he or she doesn't have to actively participate, just watch. You may offer a small reward to get him to attend enough times (say, three times) to see if he or she likes the activity. After that, your child can choose whether to continue. Sample rewards could be video game software or a music download.

3. If you are present and find the activity is not well suited to your child, you may discontinue and still give your child the reward.

HANDOUT 4.4 (continued)

AFTER TRYING THE ACTIVITY

1. Evaluate the activity:

   - Do you think your child will fit in?

   - Are other kids at the activity at the same level as your child?

   - Did you see any kids that he or she could be friends with?

   - Is the adult supervisor effective?

2. If you don't think this activity will work, try another one quickly. Repeat the steps above with the new activity.

3. Have your child evaluate the activity after the experience. Ask:

   - What did you like about the activity?

   - Were there any kids there you already knew?

   - Which kids seemed similar to you?

   - Did you have fun? Would you like to go back?

If you thought the group was not right for your child (perhaps your child was isolated or the group was unfriendly) but your child wanted to go back, have your child try another activity first before going back. He or she may have a better experience in the new activity and decide not to go back to the first one.

LESSON PLAN 4.3 Consolidating New Interests

SELECTED STUDENT NEED
- Expanding interests to attract and meet potential friends.

LEARNING OBJECTIVES
- Students with restricted interests will be able to add at least one new interest that may lead to meeting new friends.
- Students will identify activities that they have tried.

STANDARDS AND BENCHMARKS
- Try one or two new interests with parent.
- Become accurate in selecting new interests.

MATERIALS AND RESOURCES
- None

Introduction

The purpose of this class is to motivate teens to continue to try new activities.

The Class Session

Start with this introduction:

> Today we are going to continue to explore the activities we do for fun that we do with others. [Ask for a show of hands.] Who was able to try a new activity this past week that they never tried before? Who thinks they might like to go back and try that activity again? [Pick teens raising their hands to ask the following questions, which you write on the board:] (1) Did you have fun (if not, pick another activity)? (2) What did you do at the activity? (3) Was there anyone else you knew at that activity? Tell us as many details as you would like to share about this meeting. I will give you each about five minutes to talk.

Encourage the rest of the class to ask positive questions about the activity to help the teen present his interest in as good a light as possible. Then continue having teens present their interests and ask if anyone has tried a new interest that they would like to talk about.

Homework Assignment

Teens are to continue to try new activities until they have added one or two more activities they like.

Assessment

Repeat this lesson until all of the teens who are likely to try new activities have succeeded in finding new interests.

CHAPTER 5

Improving Comprehension of Figurative Language

> *Why do we say something is 'out of whack'? What is a whack?*
>
> *Why do 'slow down' and 'slow up' mean the same thing?*
>
> *Why do 'fat chance' and 'slim chance' mean the same thing?*
>
> *Why are they called 'stands' when they are made for sitting?*
>
> *Why is it called 'after dark' when it is really 'after light'?*
>
> *Why do we drive on a parkway and park on a driveway?*

In Chapter Two, we briefly discussed the difficulty that students with autism spectrum disorders have with nonliteral conversation. Their deficits are in both understanding and using nonliteral language. Most difficult for them are irony and sarcasm, since there may be no cues in the sentence (except occasionally voice tone) to reveal the speaker's intent. In contrast, many adolescents with autism spectrum disorder have little difficulty understanding similes and metaphors. Thus, we will explore where tweens and teens need the most help and focus only on idioms and sarcasm.

The lesson plans in this chapter focus on comprehension of sarcasm and idioms rather than their use. Students can probably get by adequately without using figurative speech, but their lack of comprehension is disruptive to their daily conversations.

Idioms

Of all the figures of speech, the least related to literal meaning and context is the idiom. For that reason, idioms may pose a substantial challenge to teens on the spectrum. Idioms can be used in many different situations not so much to communicate meaning as to move a conversation forward as, for example, with the idiomatic phrase, "That's how life goes sometimes." Learning idioms also poses problems for second-language learners, because idioms rarely translate verbatim from one language to another. As English as a Second Language (ESL) teachers will tell you, idioms can be effectively taught by rote learning. Consequently, there are many ESL Web sites and materials available for this purpose.

Conceptually, it is fairly simple to teach teens on the spectrum to comprehend idioms and also slang terms using rote memorization. The problem is that slang and idioms differ by region and by teen subculture, and the most common ones in daily use may be constantly changing. Thus, having an up-to-date, authoritative, and exhaustive list of idioms and slang is daunting for any book. Lesson Plan 5.1 addresses knowledge of idioms and gives students the training to search for the meaning of idioms as they hear them in conversation with peers and others.

Irony and Sarcasm

The most common forms of nonliteral speech are irony and sarcasm. Both involve statements at odds with the circumstances or statements preceding them. Ironic statements don't target a specific person and often have a humorous intent. An example of irony is the statement, "What a wonderful day for a picnic," said on a rainy day. The same statement would be an example of sarcasm if it were made to the person who had previously suggested having a picnic on that day. The intention of the person employing sarcasm can be quite varied. Sometimes it is to tease or make fun of someone, sometimes to express disapproval, and sometimes to soften a criticism (but still keep it critical). As criticism, it may add feelings such as disapproval, scorn, contempt, and ridicule to the conversation.

The use of sarcasm is not universal in all cultures. For instance, Japanese people rarely use it. Unfortunately for kids on the spectrum, it is prevalent among Americans, especially teens. One study of adults found that sarcastic remarks were used in 8 percent of conversational turns between adult friends.

Studies generally find that neurotypical children are not able to begin to comprehend sarcasm until after age six, at which time they can understand the implied meaning of the sarcastic statement. However, they don't yet understand why the speaker is using sarcasm. But even young children know something is wrong with the sarcastic statement. They often misinterpret the discrepancy between previously known facts and the intended sarcastic statement as an attempt at deception.

Understanding and the use of sarcasm is complete and, as many parents of neurotypical adolescents will tell you, fully functional by twelve years of age. This is unfortunate, for teens on the spectrum are becoming more socially aware just as this newly found skill of their neurotypical classmates is in full force. Neurotypical teens are motivated to use sarcasm in part because they feel they won't get into as much trouble as if they expressed their feelings more directly. If they are criticized for sarcastic remarks, they can claim that they truly felt what they said, even if other cues they gave off indicated something much different.

Types of Sarcasm

There are many ways to be sarcastic, although three types seem to be the most commonly employed by American English speakers. The first is understatement. An example is a parent who is chastising her son's insulting behavior with the angry statement, "That's not funny!" In fact, it was far from funny, and the voice tone and understatement are meant to emphasize the parent's annoyance. Interestingly, this parenting technique may have just the opposite effect on a younger child (and the teen on the spectrum) who doesn't understand sarcasm. It may introduce the idea that the child could be funny and perhaps should try harder to be funny.

The second form of commonly used sarcasm is overly polite sarcasm. This is also subtle because it depends in part on the relationship between speaker and listener. Consider the request, "I hate to bother you, but would you mind very much passing me the salt?" It would not qualify as sarcasm if it was said to a stranger at dinner. However, with this much politeness, if it was said to a spouse at the evening meal, it would be considered either humorous or sarcastic, depending on how happily married the spouses were. Adolescents on the spectrum are often too formal in their speech. It's as if they have a politeness rule that will keep them out of the most trouble: if they are very polite to everyone, then they will get along with the people to whom they need to be polite (strangers) and the others who don't (friends and relatives) will cut them some slack. This strategy seems to work for the most part for students on the spectrum, and they can get along without understanding more complex social relationships.

The third type of sarcasm is when the statement is meant to have a meaning opposite its literal meaning. This type is perhaps the most commonly used form of sarcasm (especially by neurotypical teens), and so much so that ESL learners are often taught about this as the only form of sarcasm that American English speakers use.

The production and comprehension rules are simple and easily taught. Thus Lesson Plan 5.2 is concerned only with this third type of sarcasm.

Recognizing Sarcasm

A speaker using sarcasm may alert listeners to his intent with nonverbal behaviors such as rolling eyes, shrugging, smirking, a sneering voice, or other features that mean, *I mean something different from what I say.* Adults can hear the message and see the nonverbal cues that modify that message and realize the speaker is being sarcastic. Nevertheless, even adult listeners sometimes have to ask, "Are you serious?" Young children and adolescents on the spectrum rely primarily on verbal messages. However, nonverbal cues do not always accompany sarcastic expression, as with the deadpan use of sarcasm (rated as funnier by most listeners who are able to pick it up). When intonation is exaggerated, studies show that younger listeners, especially by eight years of age, rate the sarcasm as "meaner" or "funnier" (funnier, that is, at the expense of the recipient).

It is more important for kids on the spectrum to recognize sarcasm and irony than to be able to use them in their conversation. Using sarcasm runs the risk of offending others. But recognizing sarcasm, especially when used on them, may alert them to a troublesome situation or a speaker who means to be hurtful. Recognition of irony and sarcasm directed at others also helps the teen maintain comprehension of the conversation.

Teaching Sarcasm and Irony

In teaching recognition of sarcasm and irony to students on the spectrum, there are three potential sources of cues:

- The context in which the sarcastic comment is made (the statement contradicts other recently made statements)
- The intonation used to make the comment (which usually involves enhanced inflection)
- Behavioral cues after the comment

The behavioral cue that neurotypical kids most commonly use is eye rolling. There are others too—for example, a speaker who says, "Nice haircut," and laughs while pointing to the recipient's head. Teaching these cues will help teens on the spectrum recognize many instances of sarcasm and irony. Remember that the more subtle the irony or sarcasm, the less likely that even neurotypical tweens and teens will recognize it.

Kids on the spectrum are at varying stages of being able to recognize sarcasm. Some don't understand the idea that speakers can use sarcasm (and thereby not mean what they are literally saying), some understand that speakers don't mean what they say but don't understand the intent of this departure (for example, that they are intending to be critical, not to lie), and some understand both of these but don't know how to respond to being criticized in this way. We focus on teaching recognition of the opposite type of sarcasm using a group session and a Socratic method.

Prior to Lesson 5.1, have each student complete Handout 5.1 in order to have a good assessment of how many idioms he knows without seeking help. Review the completed handout to divide the students into those needing help with idioms and those who have sufficient knowledge of them and can skip to other sections of this chapter.

LESSON PLAN 5.1 Learning Idioms

SELECTED STUDENT NEED

- Comprehending figurative language is a prominent conversational deficit in students with autism spectrum disorders.

LEARNING OBJECTIVES

- Students will learn common idioms.
- Students will learn to identify idioms in regular dialogue with other students and learn how to acquire their meaning without help from adults.

STANDARDS AND BENCHMARKS

- Students will systematically increase the number of correctly identified idioms.
- Students will identify and use effective strategies to identify new idioms they need to know.

MATERIALS AND RESOURCES

- List of common idioms completed prior to the beginning of the lesson. We start with eighty-six common idioms in Handout 5.1. Also consult Web sites devoted to this issue (current teen slang Web sites). Students will find these useful as well. We recommend the idiom worksheets at http://www.esl-library.com/pdf/lessons/620.type3.pdf. This site contains a collection of ESL worksheets with idioms embedded into common dialogue and the student has to find them.

Introduction

Introduce the lesson in this way: "Today we are going to learn about the more mysterious part of conversations. These are the parts that seem to make the least sense. We are going to learn how to recognize them in our conversations and how to decode them. They are called idioms and slang."

The Class Session

Review the list of common idioms during the first session. To make the discussion more interesting, have students guess how each idiom came about. Interesting or humorous stories, even if they are not accurate, may help students remember the meaning. Have them come up with a sentence to use it, and correct any inaccurate use.

Start the second session with a retest of the idiom list to assess retention. Then proceed to review the ESL worksheets, reading them together with the class. Have students volunteer to identify the embedded idiom they discovered in the text. Discuss how the idiom might have come about.

Have each student pick a reference source—for example, a dictionary of idioms and slang, a smartphone application, or a Web site—so they can look up idioms and slang they encounter in daily conversations.

Homework ssignment

Students are to bring in at least ten idioms or slang expressions to the next class. They may get a parent to help them with this assignment if you think their skills are rudimentary or that they will not be able to distinguish slang with off-color connotations. You can add more structured assignments, such as giving students a novel to read and extract idioms and slang from it. This can be an ongoing assignment in which they have to bring in ten idioms or slang words they hear each week with the definitions of each.

Assessment

Note the improvement in students' comprehension of the idioms. Many teens will begin to identify idioms in common speech and will use the resources you introduced to find meanings as the idioms come up.

Social Skills Success for Students with Autism/Asperger's, copyright © 2011 John Wiley and Sons, Inc.

HANDOUT 5.1 List of Common Idioms

1. To lend a hand.
2. In hot water.
3. Put your money where your mouth is!
4. That takes the cake!
5. Not playing with a full deck.
6. Put a lid on it!
7. Two heads are better than one!
8. To lose your shirt.
9. To lose touch.
10. Paint the town (red).
11. A picture is worth a thousand words!
12. Let's get the ball rolling!
13. I hear you!
14. You bet!
15. Once in a blue moon.
16. It's a deal!
17. To bet on the wrong horse.
18. To be full of hot air!
19. When the going gets tough, the tough get going!
20. Monkey see, monkey do!
21. To blow one's own horn.
22. Birds of a feather flock together!
23. Hit the books.
24. I can have my cake and eat it too!
25. A poker face.
26. To look like a million bucks.
27. A dime a dozen.
28. You have a one-track mind!
29. To have the inside track.
30. On the wrong side of the tracks.
31. Curiosity killed the cat!
32. The cat's out of the bag!
33. It's raining cats and dogs!
34. There's no time like the present!
35. Time heals all wounds.
36. Time out!
37. A penny for your thoughts!
38. What goes around comes around!
39. All that glitters isn't gold!
40. You scratch my back, and I'll scratch yours!
41. Rome wasn't built in a day!
42. Money talks.
43. Cat got your tongue?
44. Get in someone's hair.
45. Shoot off one's mouth.
46. Tongue-in-cheek.
47. Pull someone's leg.
48. Not have a leg to stand on.
49. Drive someone up a wall.
50. String someone along.
51. Leave someone high and dry.
52. Bend over backward.
53. Jump the gun.
54. Scratch someone's back.
55. Turn someone off.
56. Wet blanket.
57. Not out of the woods yet.
58. Eating someone up or, What's eating you?

59. Call it a day.

60. Put someone in their place.

61. Make a splash.

62. Hands are tied.

63. Catch-22.

64. Chew the fat.

65. Come clean.

66. Give someone the cold shoulder.

67. Gut feeling.

68. Answer the call of nature.

69. Brush up on.

70. To be on the safe side.

71. Double-talk.

72. In black and white.

73. Go over someone's head.

74. A peeping tom.

75. Meet someone halfway.

76. Play cat-and-mouse.

77. Top dog.

78. Back to the salt mines.

79. Get the hang of something.

80. Live in a vacuum.

81. A scandal sheet.

82. In a fix.

83. Chew the fat.

84. Bear fruit.

85. A blind alley.

86. Cock-and-bull story.

LESSON PLAN 5.2 Understanding Sarcasm

SELECTED STUDENT NEED

- Use of sarcasm is one of the defining features of early adolescence, and neurotypical teens are able to recognize and produce it. Teens with autism spectrum disorders are confronted with sarcasm in daily conversations with peers and sometimes with adults.

LEARNING OBJECTIVES

- Students will learn how to identify when their peers are making sarcastic remarks.
- Students will learn to respond appropriately to sarcastic remarks.

STANDARD AND BENCHMARK

- Use the Socratic method outlined in this lesson plan, which will present material, and then assess a student's abilities to detect sarcasm and identify the intent of the speaker.

MATERIAL AND RESOURCE

- Handout 5.2, "Examples of Sarcasm," is helpful for the lesson. It makes the contradictions inherent in sarcasm more obvious to the students: they can easily compare the sarcastic statement with the background information.

Introduction

Start by saying, "Today we are going to learn about the more mysterious parts of conversations. These are the parts that make the least sense unless you know how to decode them. We are learning about how and why people sometimes say what they don't really mean. It is not necessary for you to learn to use sarcasm, just to understand when and why someone else is using it. Many people do not like sarcasm, and it isn't that humorous. A lot of kids have fun with it, but often they are the only ones having fun. Their listeners are not."

The Class Session

After passing out Handout 5.2, ask one student to read Tom's lines and another to read James's lines. Then ask the rest of the students the questions for each of the five topics that follow (acceptable answers are in parentheses). Present the parts of sarcasm in the following order to make the presentation easier for students to understand.

LESSON PLAN 5.2 (continued)

1. Contradiction

Have students read example 1. Ask them what happened. (This is just a repeat of the story to ensure they were listening.) Ask, "What's wrong with what Tom said at the end?" (It's inconsistent with the information we are given at the beginning. If students don't understand, read the example again, this time pointing out the contradiction.) Ask, "Did Tom mean to thank James?" (No.) "Why did he say that?" (He wanted to show James that he was annoyed. Don't accept answers like, "He was lying," or "He was trying to deceive James.") "Does anyone know what this is called?" (Sarcasm.) "Tom was actually criticizing James. Does everyone see that? The way he said it was meant to show James that he was annoyed and to make James feel bad about not helping. If he had said, 'I wish you had helped me more,' he wouldn't have been showing that he was upset."

2. Target

Have students read example 2. Ask them what happened. (It's a repeat of the story to ensure they were listening.) Ask, "What's wrong with what Tom said at the end?" (It's inconsistent with the information we are given at the beginning.) Ask, "Did Tom mean that the weather was nice?" (No.) "Why did he say that?" (To be mildly funny.) "Notice the difference between examples 1 and 2. Which one is funnier?" (Example 2.) "Why?" (Example 2 doesn't try to make anyone feel bad. It doesn't target anyone.) "Example 2 is an example of irony."

3. Speaker's Intent

Have students read example 3. Explain to them that sarcasm is hard to understand, and many people miss it. The person who is sarcastic wants others to know he doesn't mean what he says. Otherwise they won't understand the point they are trying to make. Ask, "What is Tom also trying to get James to understand about his feelings?" (Tom is annoyed or upset that James got him to agree to play baseball.)

4. Extra Cues: Eye Roll, Voice Tone, Laughing, and Pointing

Take Tom's part in example 4. Announce that you are going to read this twice. On the first reading, say, "Fine," in a neutral voice, with no facial expression. The second time, say, "Fine," while rolling your eyes and using a sarcastic tone. Then ask students what happened. (It's just a repeat of the story to ensure they were listening.) Ask, "What's wrong with what Tom said at the end?" (It's inconsistent with the information we are given at the beginning, that is, he didn't really want to sit by the door.) "What unusual thing did Tom do as he spoke?" (He rolled his eyes.) "Why did he do that?" (To show sarcasm.) Ask, "Did Tom mean that

Social Skills Success for Students with Autism/Asperger's, copyright © 2011 John Wiley and Sons, Inc.

LESSON PLAN 5.2   (continued)

sitting by the door was okay with him?" (No. His use of the word *Fine* meant, "I will reluctantly consent, but *not* with pleasure.") "If Tom was really agreeable to sitting by the door, he would have said a lot more to show it—for example, 'That's fine with me.' So why did he roll his eyes and use a sarcastic tone?" (To make James feel bad about getting his way.). "Notice that Tom says exactly the same thing both times we read example 4. What's the difference between 'Fine' [saying it with a neutral tone] and 'Fine' [saying it with rolling eyes and sarcastic intonation]?" (The second is "meaner" than the first. Tom is angrier in the second example.) End up in this way: "See how the eyes and voice tone make a difference? Rolling eyes almost always means sarcasm. The word *Fine* almost always means sarcasm. Using them both helps to make sure that more people will understand that sarcasm is being used."

Read the other two examples and have students discuss them to ensure that they understand sarcasm.

5. Extra Cues for Electronic Communication

Say, "On the Web, it is impossible to tell if someone is being sarcastic unless they tell you that's what they are doing. But there is no universal sign for sarcasm. The section at the end of the handout shows how people try to tell you they are using irony or sarcasm on the Web." Then explain each of the examples in Handout 5.2.

6. How People Use Sarcasm on the Web

It's hard enough for many people to understand that others are using sarcasm when they are speaking. It's almost impossible when they are communicating on the Web. The handout has some signs people put at the end of sentences to let others know they are using sarcasm.

Homework Assignment

Students are to bring to the next class at least five examples of sarcasm or irony they heard in conversation. They may get parent help with this assignment if you feel that their skills are rudimentary or they cannot yet distinguish sarcasm. You can also add more structured assignments, such as assigning a novel for students to read and extract sarcasm.

Assessment

Note students' improvement in identification and comprehension of sarcasm and the speaker's intent.

Example 1: Contradiction

Tom and James were given a project by their teacher to do together. They met at the library and were supposed to work together. Tom worked all day on the school project while James just played video games. When Tom finished the project he turned to James and said, "Thanks for the help."

Example 2: Target

Tom and James both wanted to play basketball outside but can't now because it's raining very hard and the basketball court is wet. Tom turns to James and says, "Nice weather we're having."

Example 3: Speaker's Intent

It was James's idea to play basketball, and Tom reluctantly agreed. They can't now because it's raining very hard and the basketball court is wet. Tom turns to James and says, "Nice weather we're having."

Example 4: Extra Cues

Tom and James want to sit together at lunch in the cafeteria. Tom wants to sit next to a window, but James says, "There's too much light there. Why don't we sit by the door?" Tom says, "Fine."

Example 5

James borrows Tom's unopened container of milk and pours almost all of it over his small bowl of cereal. Tom says to James, "Would you like some cereal with your milk?"

Example 6

James is wearing a striped shirt and pants with polka dots. Upon first seeing him that day, Tom says to James, "Nice outfit!"

Example 7: Examples of Sarcasm and Irony on the Web

Nice weather we're having ;)
Nice weather we're having ☺
Nice weather we're having ~
Nice weather we're having. lol
Nice weather we're having (^/end sarcasm)
NICE weather we're having

Social Skills Success for Students with Autism/Asperger's, copyright © 2011 John Wiley and Sons, Inc.

CHAPTER 6

Improving Conversational Comprehension

> *You're not given much time to consider the meaning of something you hear in a conversation. I often feel pressured to respond to a comment made by someone in a timely fashion. A few seconds later, I'll become aware of something that changes the entire meaning of what they just said.*

Students with autism spectrum disorders usually demonstrate large spoken vocabularies and generally intact formal language skills. However, they have difficulty with many aspects of conversational dynamics and content. One challenge they have is initiating topics of shared interest to a conversational partner. Once a topic is introduced, they then have difficulty staying on this topic (unless, of course, it is one of their restricted interests). Some clinicians feel that this is due to an inability to understand what the conversational partner already knows and is thinking about, as well as what the partner wishes to know. However, research on theory of mind indicates that by the time high-functioning students with autism spectrum disorders are teenagers, most are able to figure out what others know. Evidence from our work indicates that kids with autism lack two basic types of skills that impair comprehension: skills that ensure they understand everything that was said and skills to discern the goals of specific conversations.

The primary focus for this chapter is teaching tweens and teens how to ensure they comprehend what was said and how to give feedback about this. Improving the conversational skills of teens with autism spectrum disorders is crucial for them to be integrated into the mainstream of school life.

We will not address issues of eye contact during conversations, a common component of many interventions that address conversational skills. Studies have shown that many children and low-functioning teens on the spectrum have unusual gaze. They often focus on irrelevant aspects of a picture presented to them. This behavior is almost never present in teens who are high functioning, and, in fact, even neurotypical teenage boys usually avert their gaze. Fleeting gaze is more the norm for neurotypical boys, while constant, unfaltering gaze is more the norm for neurotypical girls. Teaching more constant eye contact to teenage boys on the spectrum may be teaching them to make other boys feel uncomfortable. Thus, we have deliberately omitted focus on eye contact from the conversational skills addressed in this chapter.

Goals of Conversations

It's useful to think of conversations between adolescents and adults as being guided by the goals each individual brings to the conversation. Many of the conversational problems of kids on the spectrum result from a lack of understanding of these goals, which guide both of the conversational partners to stay on track. The conversational goals can also guide subsequent conversations. If conversational partners quickly collaborate on their goals at the beginning of the conversation, the conversation has a better chance of going more smoothly. This collaboration helps conversational partners form expectations of the kinds of topics their partner is interested in for future conversations.

Two general kinds of goals guide conversations between two individuals: task-oriented goals, for when they are working together to accomplish tasks, and social goals, for when they are focused more on each other's emotional needs. Usually each kind of conversation includes elements of the other. Conversations with primarily social goals are different from conversations with primarily task-oriented goals in two respects:

- Conversations with task-oriented goals are focused on more observable actions and objects, while the focus of social conversations is more ambiguous.

- The goals of a task-oriented conversation are initially made explicit, while goals of a social conversation are almost never explicitly stated.

Because the goals of task-oriented conversations are not only more concrete and observable and the conversational goals are explicitly stated by one or both conversational partners, it makes sense to teach skills for this kind of conversation first. Two skills are important to teach: checking for accuracy and repairing comprehension problems (known as conversational repair). Both of these are important skills that address deficits in teens on the spectrum (they are also helpful in conversations with social goals, which we discuss in the next chapter). Many high-functioning teens on the spectrum by now have acquired prerequisite cognitive skills so that they are ready to learn some simple rules that will improve their conversations.

Ensuring Mutual Understanding

Words and phrases in conversation are often misunderstood by neurotypical conversational partners. Miscommunication can have more devastating effects for task-oriented conversations than social conversations. A prime example was the 1999 loss of a $125 million NASA Mars orbiter. The mission failed because one engineering team used metric units and failed to communicate this to another team, which used English units for a key space-craft operation. Neurotypical people have learned to employ techniques devoted to effective task-oriented conversations so as to take account of this phenomenon. Rather than just assuming that the other has understood what he or she has said, the neurotypical speaker often waits for an acknowledg-ment from the listener. In task-oriented conversation, there are more pauses to ensure that mutual understanding is continuing to occur. The pauses allow accuracy checks from the listener and may help teens on the spectrum who are often overwhelmed by the speed of conversation.

Task-oriented conversations should contain accuracy checks that ensure that both parties understand everything that is said. Accuracy checks, such as "yes," "I understand," "okay," "right," and "uh-huh," are common responses that are effective in acknowledging comprehension. Some acknowledgments are made with these statements and some by continuing with the next relevant response (for example, an answer to a question), some by paraphrasing what the speaker has just said, and some by visual cues, such as head nodding or continued eye contact. Using accuracy checks fosters a more engaged conversation and may slow down the conversation, which may also be helpful to teens on the spectrum. These responses are listed in the first part of Handout 6.1

Conversational Repair Strategies

Another strategy people use to ensure mutual understanding in a conver-sation is to use statements that initiate repair when mutual understanding breaks down. If they cannot understand what is being said to them, they seek clarification and try to work things out. People are usually very good at noticing when a conversation has gone awry because one party has not communicated effectively with the other. This starts them figuring out the exact nature of the problem and selecting the right response to recover from the error.

There are two types of communication breakdowns: *not understanding*, meaning the listener and speaker know that the listener did not make sense of the last utterance, and *misunderstanding*, when the listener interprets the utterance incorrectly and doesn't know the interpretation is not the one the speaker intended. Here is an example of a misunderstanding:

Rachel: Do you know who's got Mrs. Cummings for history?
Sarah: Who?
Rachel: I don't know.
Sarah: Oh. I think Steve and also George.

Although Rachel asked a question, Sarah initially thought Rachel knew the answer. Rachel repaired the error with "I don't know." Sarah then quickly realized her misunderstanding. As you can see, repairing a misunderstanding is a sophisticated skill that cannot be easily taught and will not be addressed in this book. A few common repair strategies are also listed in Handout 6.1. Using these will substantially improve the conversational comprehension of teens on the spectrum.

Teaching Better Task-Oriented Conversations, Accuracy Checks, and Repair Statements

Lesson Plan 6.1 includes some nonsense drawings at the end of the plan that pairs of teens will use in a communication game. The game structure is designed to promote all the skills that are being worked on. The game can be played several times with each pair of students to allow adequate practice. Eventually the teacher may want to substitute academic tasks that are more typically done in groups to promote further generalization of the skills.

Accuracy checks and repair statements give students an acceptable means to stay engaged in a conversation. Students on the spectrum are more likely to stay on topic because they are more active participants and don't allow themselves to get lost in any part of the conversation. Many have become used to losing the drift of the meaning of conversations and have learned to live with this. Now they are introduced to a higher standard of communication, where they don't lose the meaning.

LESSON PLAN 6.1 Accuracy Checks and Repair in Conversations

Social Skills Success for Students with Autism/Asperger's, copyright © 2011 John Wiley and Sons, Inc.

SELECTED STUDENT NEED

- Improving conversational skills for students with autism spectrum disorders is crucial for them to become integrated into the mainstream of school life. This lesson addresses the student's inability to address conversational breakdowns, when meaning has been lost between conversational partners. It focuses on conversational repair and accuracy checking skills. Using these skills will enhance the amount of social learning that teens with autism spectrum disorders can get for themselves in future social interactions with peers.

LEARNING OBJECTIVES

- Students will learn effective ways to alert their conversational partner that they continue to understand the meaning of the conversation.

- Students will learn techniques for conversational repair when they don't understand a speaker's intended meaning.

STANDARDS AND BENCHMARKS

- Use an initial conversational exchange between two students to assess each student's use of accuracy checks and conversational repair.

- By the conclusion of this lesson, assess students for improvement in the use of both conversational skills.

MATERIALS AND RESOURCES

- Enough photocopied sets of nonsense drawings to supply each student in the class with a complete set (see Figure 6.1). The drawings should be individually cut out, so that they can be arranged in any order.

- Handout 6.1, "Skills to Help You Understand More of a Conversation"

Introduction

Introduce the lesson in this way:

> Today we are going to learn how to make sure we understand all parts of conversations that we participate in. We will learn how to let each other know when we *do* understand. That's called an accuracy check. And we will learn how to get the information we need to keep understanding. That's called a repair question.

LESSON PLAN 6.1 (continued)

Every conversation should have at least one goal. Let's suppose we have to get something done that also includes someone else. Let's suppose we have a conversation while we are getting it done. What do you think the one important goal of our conversation would be?

Use the Socratic method to get students to voice the goal. Accept, "To make sure both people do the task the correct way," as the best answer.

The Class Session

1. Pass out Handout 6.1. Continue using the Socratic method to review each of the accuracy checks in the handout as follows. First, instruct one of the students to get up in front of the class and give you directions to some geographical place she knows. Then instruct her to stop after each sentence. After the first pause, say that you understood what the student said. Ask, "How could I briefly let the speaker know that I understood?" and then quickly add, "What's wrong with saying nothing?" Next, "Look at the list of accuracy checks on the handout and tell me what things I can say to let him know I understand his directions." After the first response, say, "That's what we call an accuracy check." Have a student read aloud the first part of Handout 6.1. Then have this student pick one of the responses to use as an accuracy check and model it with the student you are getting directions from. After each sentence, repeat this, having students pick another response from the handout.

2. Break students into pairs, and have them practice this with each other: one student gives the other directions to a place they both know. Make sure the speaker pauses after each sentence. Each student should have a turn as the speaker and the listener using validating phrases for about five minutes.

3. Next review the "repair" sentences. Have one student read each repair question on the handout and give an example of each. Instruct another student to get up in front of the class and give you directions to some place he knows, with pauses after each sentence. Now tell the group that you didn't understand the whole sentence and ask them what you should do next. Ask them what is wrong with not doing anything and letting the student continue with directions. On the next sentence, tell the students you didn't understand one word (pick a specific word in the sentence). Ask what you should do. Repeat this until you have covered each repair response in the handout.

4. Again break students into pairs, and have them practice this sort of conversation with each other.

5. Next, have the students play the nonsense drawings game. Pass out the set of nonsense drawings to each student, and break the students into pairs. Instruct them as follows:

> I want you to hide these drawings from each other. I want one person in each pair to pick seven drawings out of all of them. Now put them in an order you like, but don't tell or show your partner the order and the drawings you pick. [Wait for all the students to do this.] Your task is to have your partner pick the same nonsense drawings as you did and arrange their sets of nonsense drawings in the same order as you. You are to have them do so only by talking to them. Your partner is not to see your figures. In order to do this, you will have to come up with descriptions of each nonsense drawing. For example, I can describe this drawing [showing the third drawing on the bottom line in Figure 6.1] as a semicircle with a "W" and a plus sign. Let's see who finishes first using the tools we have just learned to make sure we understand. Be sure to use accuracy checks when you do understand and repair questions when you don't.

Homework Assignment

Assign students in pairs to call each other to practice the nonsense drawing game at home. Have them pick a time to call each other before leaving class. Also tell them to have their parents read the handout and listen to this game to give them help. Students should show Handout 6.1 to their parent before practicing. They should take the drawings home and continue to play the game with each other over the telephone in order to promote generalization of skills.

The telephone call between students should be prearranged so that parents are present during the entire call. Parents should be ready to step in if the teens doing the assignment miss the opportunity for an accuracy check or repair statement.

Assessment

Follow up in the next session to see if the students did the homework. Ask for specific details about other times during the week when they used these techniques and what the conversation was about. Ask if the techniques helped them. Note the improvement in the use of accuracy checks and repair statements.

Social Skills Success for Students with Autism/Asperger's, copyright © 2011 John Wiley and Sons, Inc.

FIGURE 6.1 Nonsense Drawings

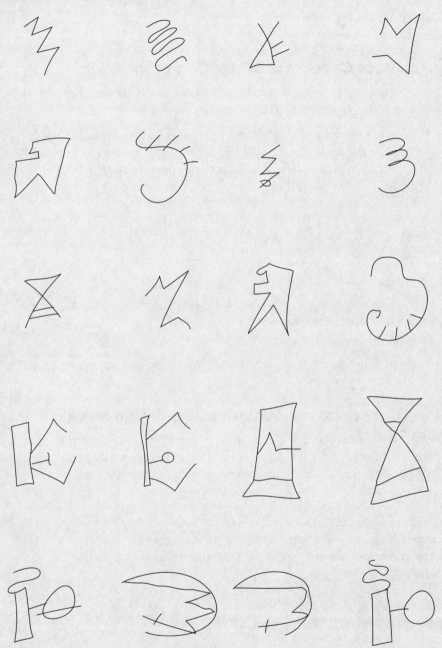

Using Accuracy Checks for Better Comprehension

Everyone sometimes has trouble understanding what someone else is saying to them. It happens to all of us, and it happens often.

You can tell a speaker that you understand what he is saying. In fact, this is essential when you are working on a task together. Here are some words you can use after waiting for a pause to indicate it's your turn to speak:

- I understand.
- Yes.
- Okay.
- Right.
- Uh-huh.

Most people like to hear these words when they are trying to get you to understand something. It also helps slow down what they are saying so you are better able to understand.

You can also nod your head. This is a good response because it doesn't interrupt the person who is telling you something.

Repairing Conversations When You Don't Understand

When people don't understand, they use a code to get the other person to help them **repair** the conversation. It's a code that a lot of people know and use. If you don't understand, here are some things you can say to have the other person help you out:

You can: Say, "Huh?" or "What?"
This means: You didn't understand the whole last sentence.
What the other person will probably do next: Repeat the whole sentence.

You should not use this too often because this is usually too much work for the other speaker and may get him frustrated.

You can: Ask a "Who...," "Where...," or "When..." question.
This means: You have figured out which part of the sentence you don't understand.
What the other person will probably do next: Repeat the relevant part of the sentence.

HANDOUT 6.1 (continued)

This makes it much easier for the other speaker to help you because you have done some of the work.

> **You can:** Take a guess and say, "You mean..."
>
> **This means:** You heard one or more words in the sentence that you didn't understand.
>
> **What the other person will probably do next:** Correct you if she didn't mean that and use a different word in that part of the sentence or agree with you if you were correct.

Saying this tells the speaker that you are trying to understand. She will be more sympathetic to the question unless you think you will usually guess incorrectly. Guessing incorrectly may frustrate the speaker.

> **You can:** Repeat the word or part of the sentence you didn't understand as a question.
>
> **This means:** You heard one or more words in the sentence but didn't understand.
>
> **What the other person will probably do next:** Rephrase the part of the sentence you didn't understand.

This is usually a good response. It is easy on the speaker, and you don't have to take wild guesses.

> **You can:** Say, "Could you explain what ... means?"
>
> **This means:** You heard a word or words in the sentence but didn't understand.
>
> **What the other person will probably do next:** Rephrase that part of the sentence you didn't understand.

This is usually a good thing to say. It is easy on the speaker and you don't have to take a wild guess.

Caution: Don't repeat the same question if it was already answered unless you didn't hear the answer.

Special note to parents helping with this homework assignment: Please read this handout. If you decide to help your child with these skills, have him or her practice accuracy checking and repair questions by picking seven of the nonsense drawings. Then have your child call his or her assigned partner. Have the kids take turns trying to guess which drawings were picked and in what order. Be ready to step in and remind your child if he or she forgets either an accuracy check or a repair statement.

CHAPTER 7

Improving Social Conversations

> *We visited Hollywood, through the town of Westlake. We took the Metro Red line. We stopped at Civic Center, Pershing Square, Seventh Street Metro Center, MacArthur Park, Wilshire/Vermont, Vermont Beverly, Vermont/Santa Monica, Vermont/Sunset, Hollywood/Western and Hollywood/Vine. We arrived at 10:42. Then we went on a tour of Hollywood on the Star Line transportation bus, like my school bus, which goes down Old Country Road where James lives and then on to Oyster Bay Road before it comes to our school. We saw lots of things like Grauman's Chinese theater. The tour ended at 2:37, and then we went home.*

Teens with autism spectrum disorder differ in terms of how interested they are in social contacts. One would expect from the description of symptoms of the disorder that there would be a high proportion of these kids who are classically introverted, and a study of adults indeed reported that the incidence of introversion was higher in the sample of adults with autism spectrum disorder than in a sample of neurotypical adults. However, only 35 percent of adults on the spectrum were in the range of what might be termed introverts (as opposed to 4 percent of the control group). Thus, it appears that many or most teens on the spectrum want to have social contacts.

Potential Understanding of Conversational Goals

A study presented high-functioning students on the spectrum with pictures of a lone child next to other children playing a game. The students were able to discern that the lone child wanted to meet the other children. However, most could not figure out the steps the child could take to accomplish this.

These studies mesh with our experience that students on the spectrum have both the desire and sufficient cognitive development to potentially understand much of the social world they have been missing. In particular they are able to learn more about having social conversations than they already know.

Social conversations present particular challenges for many students on the spectrum. The goals of social conversations are more ambiguous than task-oriented conversations because the goals are almost never explicitly stated and there are usually no tangibles involved. Social goals may range from the immediate, such as enjoyment of a social interaction or making a favorable impression, to longer-term goals such as the development of relationships or self-esteem. Responses need to be appropriate, but fortunately they do not need to be ideal to meet conversational goals. This all sounds overwhelmingly complicated, but there are actually only four general goals for initial social conversations. Friendly social conversations usually have these goals:

- Making the listener and the speaker feel good about themselves (enhancing self-esteem)
- Communicating liking for one another without saying it directly

- Assessing the other person's interest in you

- Presenting oneself as friendly

Social conversations are often entertaining without deliberate attempts to be so.

Pleasant conversations with social goals require the cooperation of both partners in four domains:

- *Cooperative agreement on the goals of the conversation.* These are quickly established at the beginning. The goals of each partner don't have to be the same, but both must agree to them for the conversation to be pleasant.

- *The flow of a conversation.* Topic shifts must be small enough to maintain continuity, with occasional larger shifts to establish new directions.

- *Control of topic direction.* When partners share the control of direction, the experience is more pleasant for both partners.

- *Cooperative involvement with frequent accuracy checks while a partner is making an extended contribution to the conversation.* This uses the same accuracy checks and repair statements as we presented for task-oriented conversations in the last chapter. Thus, the accuracy checks and repair statements we discussed in the previous chapter also come in handy for social conversations.

Small Talk

Kids on the spectrum frequently overlook small talk because its purpose eludes them. Nevertheless, small talk has specific and important goals. It helps people who barely know each other to show that they have friendly intentions and perhaps a desire for some sort of positive interaction. It gives them the opportunity to test the receptivity of a possible conversational partner to start a conversation or just establish equality. It is also a helpful beginning to a conversation between people who know each other better because it serves as a gentle way to eventually get down to business and puts people at ease. Thus, one of the goals of Lesson Plan 7.1 is to have tweens and teens on the spectrum understand the purpose of small talk and become comfortable in using it and decoding the information it provides.

Using small talk is one way that teens on the spectrum can be more cautious in their friendship overtures to peers. And teens who approach others cautiously are more likely to be successful in relating to peers.

Parts of Conversations

Most social conversations have distinct parts. They usually start with a hello and sometimes the question, "How are you?" which usually evokes a one- or two-word response and a reciprocal, "How are you?" The speakers sometimes have a cover story (an excuse for starting the conversation) for the conversation (which may or may not be the actual goal) and is usually mentioned at first. The body of the conversation is next. Then there is an ending cover story, usually a time constraint or some other reason to gracefully end the conversation. Sometimes a long pause serves to initiate this ending cover story. The conversation ends with the farewell statement, "See you soon" or "It's been nice talking to you." The lesson plan presents the parts of a conversation in a format in which teens on the spectrum can begin to understand.

LESSON PLAN 7.1 Having a Social Conversation

SELECTED STUDENT NEEDS

- Improving conversational skills for students with autism spectrum disorders is crucial for being integrated into the mainstream of school life.
- This lesson also addresses the inability of students on the spectrum to respond to or make small talk. This inability may send a message of social awkwardness and may make others uncomfortable, which can be avoided by teaching this simple skill.

LEARNING OBJECTIVES

- Students will learn parts of a conversation.
- Students will learn how to respond to and use small talk.

STANDARDS AND BENCHMARKS

- Assess a student's knowledge about small talk and conversational goals by asking questions.
- At the conclusion of this lesson, assess students for improvement in the use of small talk and conversational goals.

MATERIAL AND RESOURCE

- Handout 7.1, "Parts of a Conversation"

Introduction

Begin the lesson with, "Today we are going to learn how to handle different conversations and the parts of conversations. Thinking about these parts may help us organize our thoughts better and help make everyone in the conversation feel more comfortable."

The Class Session

1. Pass out Handout 7.1. Then say:

   Let's read the first conversation between Joe and Ted. People are always asking each other, "How are you?" Does anyone know why we do it? [Have students read aloud the "Goals of a Conversation" section. Then say:] Usually "How are you?" questions are not what they seem. Which of the goals listed in the handout do you think the "How are you?" question usually has? [Wait for answers from the students.] One of the first two goals on the handout is most often the goal of "How are you?" People feel very uncomfortable asking, "Do you want to talk to me?" So they ask how the other person is. This question can make the other person feel good that someone else is interested in them, so if they even slightly want to talk to you, you have made them feel more comfortable and they might want to talk even more. Fortunately, this type of conversation comes up a lot and the goals are always similar. Once you know what the goals are, this conversation can be very useful.

2. Now show the class how the "How are you?" exchange can be the only conversation by rereading Joe and Ted's exchange and have both characters say good-bye to each other.

3. Now you are about to review all of the parts of a conversation with students. Read parts 1 and 2 of the handout.

4. In the second sample conversation in part 2 in the handout, Eric was not interested in conversing at the moment. Have students notice how he said good-bye instead of continuing the conversation. Tell students that is something they can do in the same way when they can't or don't want to speak to someone. The "How are you?" exchange lets them do it quickly without hurting the other person's feelings, when their voice tone is pleasant.

5. Now have one teen play Sam and you play Eric. Read that same exchange in part 2 again. The first time, you (as Eric) cheerfully answer. Ask the students if Eric likes Sam and is interested in talking to him. Then say to them, "This time Eric will like Sam and will be interested in talking to him. But listen how he answers and tell me what's wrong with the way he answers." This time use a very flat affect and constantly glance away. Ask them why it didn't seem that Eric was much interested in Sam or his conversation.

6. Ask if Sam should continue the conversation. Ask what signs there would be that Sam was uncomfortable or comfortable and maybe wanted to talk more (or not).

7. Have students pair up to practice the "How are you?" exchange as correctly as they can. Accept and praise any improvement in voice tone.

8. Now read part 3 of the handout, "The Body of the Conversation." Ask what the goals of the conversation were. The answer is, "To show that they are friendly, talk about golf, and see if they have a mutual interest in golf."

Social Skills Success for Students with Autism/Asperger's copyright © 2011 John Wiley and Sons, Inc.

9. Now say, "Okay, at what point do Sam and Eric figure out what the goal of their conversation is?" Read the conversation in part 3 of the handout aloud to them and stop at each line. Take a longer pause at about the ninth line and ask, "What about now? Have they agreed on the goal of this conversation?" (The answer is, "Yes. They both agreed to talk about golf.")

10. Have students notice that both Sam and Eric are adding extra information to their answers. This also indicates that they are interested in talking to each other.

11. Read steps 4 and 5 in the handout and point out the pause in Eric and Sam's conversation. Point out how the conversation ended.

12. Pair students, and have them practice conversations with each other. Before they start, have one of each pair pick one of the four goals for their conversation and tell you what it will be. Tell them to converse for about five minutes and then end the conversation. You may have to prompt them to end the conversations with an excuse for ending and a farewell (steps 4 and 5). After ten minutes, have each member of the pair say what the goal of the conversation was.

Homework Assignment

Have students try these techniques at school and report back at the next session.

Assessment

Repeat this practice as necessary until students demonstrate they understand all parts of a conversation. Follow up in the next session to see if they did the homework.

HANDOUT 7.1 Parts of a Conversation

THE "HOW ARE YOU?" CONVERSATION

> *Joe:* How are you?
> *Ted:* I'm fine. How are you?
> *Joe:* I'm fine. Thanks for asking!

Goals of a Conversation

Before you start a conversation, think first about your goal for the conversation. Is it:

- To find out how much someone wants to talk to you?
- To show that you are friendly?
- To work something out?
- To find out what happened to the other person recently?
- To see how something you did together with them is turning out?
- To arrange getting together (if the person knows you and you have gotten together before)?

Parts of a Conversation

A complete conversation has five parts (not all conversations are complete):

1. Hello

It's always okay to say hello.

2. The "How Are You?" Exchange

Here's how the exchange goes:

> *Sam:* Hello.
> *Eric:* Oh, hello, Sam. How are you?
> *Sam:* Fine, thanks. How are you?
> *Eric:* Fine!

This part of the conversation lets you see if the other person is receptive to talking more or whether the other person has something to say to you first.

If the other person is in a hurry or doesn't want to talk to you, he or she can end the conversation now to let you know this isn't a good time to talk. Sam appears to like talking to Eric. If he didn't or was in a hurry, he could have just said, "Fine, thanks," at the end and could have started walking away.

Social Skills Success for Students with Autism/Asperger's, copyright © 2011 John Wiley and Sons, Inc.

HANDOUT 7.1 (continued)

Here is a sample conversation in which Eric doesn't want to continue:

> *Sam:* Hello.
> *Eric:* Oh, hello, Sam. How are you?
> *Sam:* Fine, thanks. How was your weekend?
> *Eric:* It was great! How was yours?
> *Sam:* Mine was great too. Did you get out at all? [Sam asks a question to keep the conversation going.]
> *Eric:* Not much. I had too much to do. I gotta get going. Nice talking to you! [Eric has to go.]
> *Sam:* Same here. Catch you later!

3. The Body of the Conversation

If you get to this part of the conversation:

- Remember your accuracy checking and repair statements if you didn't understand something.

- Don't change the subject unless there is a long pause. Sometimes a long pause indicates you are done with your goals.

Here is a sample conversation in which both Sam and Eric want to talk (about golf):

> *Sam:* Hello.
> *Eric:* Oh, hello, Sam. How are you?
> *Sam:* Fine, thanks. How was your weekend?
> *Eric:* It was great! How was yours?
> *Sam:* Mine was great too. Did you get out at all? [Sam asks a question to keep the conversation going.]
> *Eric:* Yes, I played some golf. [Eric helps to keep the conversation going.]
> *Sam:* Golf! What course?
> *Eric:* Mar Vista. It's near my house.
> *Sam:* I've never been to Mar Vista Golf Course. Is it good to play on?
> *Eric:* They were working on the ninth hole.
> *Sam:* Oh, you should try Del Rey. It's not too far.
> *Eric:* Thanks for the tip.
> *Sam:* Don't mention it. [Longer pause; they are finished talking about golf.]
> *Eric:* Well, got to get to class.
> *Sam:* It was nice talking to you. Take care!
> *Eric:* Thanks. I'll see you!

4. An Excuse for Ending

It is always better to excuse yourself rather than skipping directly to the farewell.
Here are two examples:

- "Well, I've got to get to class."
- "Well, I've got to start my homework."

5. The Farewell

Here are two examples:

- "See you!" You can insert an approximate or definite arranged time, but it's not necessary.
- "It's been nice talking to you."

Notes:

CHAPTER 8

Helping Students Choose Friends

> *Nick is in the school band. He quickly gets the melody on the trombone the first time. Band has allowed him to be part of a group. Some other band members are also eccentric, so he is able to blend in.*

Students with autism spectrum disorders who are either partially or fully included in regular classrooms are likely to have a strong desire to fit into the mainstream of school life. But many of their classmates view their behaviors as odd, eccentric, and peculiar. Studies of the few students on the spectrum who are more successful at fitting in indicate that they use cautious social approaches and bids for friendship.

Thus far, we have discussed fitting into the academic life of middle and high school. This chapter reviews the best approaches for teachers to help students on the spectrum meet potential friends. In addition to the lessons in the previous chapters in Part Two, most teens will need formal social skills training such as the PEERS program in order for these efforts to pay off. The peer mentor program described in Chapter Twelve is a helpful adjunct for helping them fit in, as are the lesson plans described in Chapter Ten, which describe how teachers and educators can help kids on the spectrum deal with meltdowns that interfere with their social functioning.

Neurotypical Teen Relationships

In Chapter One, we reviewed the more global challenges that neurotypical teens face as they grow up. Now we look closely at the development of their closer relationships. We made the point in Chapter One that neurotypical kids form crowds that are identified by mutual interests, dress, musical tastes, and leisure activities, and they draw their best friends from members of their crowd. Thus, even neurotypical adolescents are not universally accepted by all other adolescents. The PEERS program addresses this issue by guiding parents and teens to find an appropriate crowd from which to draw friendships.

We define a best friendship as a mutual relationship, formed with affection and commitment, between individuals who consider themselves equals. The most enduring outcome of preadolescence is the development of close friendships. Having one or two best friends is of great importance to later adjustment, can buffer the impact of stressful events, and correlates positively with self-esteem and negatively with anxious and depressive symptoms in later life. Best friends promote the development of social competence. Whereas conflicts between acquaintances can inhibit future social interaction, studies show that conflicts between best friends and their resolution are associated with subsequent increases in social problem-solving abilities. Thus, the best friend is a confidant who teaches important social skills as students grow up together.

A friendship has four main qualities that are not characteristic of other relationships: companionship, support, intimacy, and trust:

- Companionship for tweens and teens means there is someone with whom to hang out.
- Support can consist of having someone with whom they can share their thoughts and feelings (emotional support) and having someone they can rely on for help when they need it (instrumental support).
- Having an intimate friend means there is someone with whom they can share their thoughts, feelings, and experiences.
- Trusting the other person with their secrets and feelings strengthens intimacy.

The visible features of friendship—doing things together, having similar behaviors and preferences, and liking and being liked—develop before adolescence. The deeper qualities of friendship begin to appear during adolescence: having relationships with trust, support, and intimacy.

Although school is a common meeting ground for forming new friendships, a deeper friendship is one that transcends the school situation. The fact that someone else will exert extra effort to get together outside the original meeting place is a self-esteem boost that deepens the relationship. Thus, teens must have skills to turn at least some school friends into friends in other contexts, such as home, neighborhood, and extracurricular activity. Stories abound of teens on the spectrum who have friends only at school. This becomes an acute problem when they graduate from high school and have no one with whom to get together. Some teens, both neurotypical and those on the spectrum, may not get together with friends outside school; they lack the confidence to ask, are unsure of how to extend and accept invitations, or don't know which classmates to approach. These are important gaps in their skills to address.

Friends of Teens with Autism Spectrum Disorders

The school environment, inclusive or segregated, has large effects on the types and qualities of friendships of teens on the spectrum. Many higher-functioning teens prefer more inclusive school situations, whereas others may prefer separate school environments because they feel less different and more comfortable with peers like them.

Although many high-functioning teens had major difficulties with friendships when younger, many report having at least one friend by the time they reach adolescence. Those more likely to report having a friend have less social impairment. However, research studies find that having this friend does not necessarily lessen the usually great feelings of loneliness these young people have. We suspect that these friendships are of poor quality. Studies indicate that many kids on the spectrum feel loneliness less as a feeling of sadness and more from their knowledge of being excluded and missing out on the neurotypical teen experience. One study showed that social support from parents, classmates, and best friends helped to decrease loneliness somewhat, but many kids on the spectrum still long for friendships with neurotypical teens.

We are just beginning to understand the closer friendships of teens on the spectrum. These friendships have been noted to be centered on the teens' special interests (such as computer games and video games) or activities that require minimal social interactions such as walking or exercising. After-school social contacts between teens on the spectrum typically consist of getting together to play video games, with little conversational exchange, and then ending when the games are completed and the guest leaves (although this depends on the type of friend). These friendships are often facilitated and supervised by adults. The teens themselves rate this typical get-together without significant conversation as a poor-quality friendship.

Some of our ideas about what to aim for in friendships of kids on the spectrum come from studies of students with disabilities, which usually include teens on the spectrum. Therefore, the methods set out in this chapter are a best guess and may need to be modified as research on teens on the spectrum continues. There are differences in interview studies noted between students with disabilities and neurotypical students in what they consider the important qualities of friendships. Students with disabilities stressed the importance of helpfulness in friendship, whereas neurotypical students stressed intimacy. Important qualities of friends reported by students with disabilities were (in order of frequency of reports) that they did things with each other, they saw them in more than one location, they shared interests with their friends, and they were friends for a long time. Intimacy was not high on this list as it would be for neurotypical teens. But arranging home get-togethers between classmates was important for teens with disabilities.

The Internet and Friendships

It has been argued that the Internet may be particularly beneficial for students on the spectrum in order to help them make and sustain friendships. The reasoning is that using electronic media may mask communication problems that teens on the spectrum have. For instance, there's no body language or voice tone in electronic communication, so deficits in understanding do not handicap students on the spectrum. But this logic has two problems. First, previous research has found that students on the spectrum were more likely to use the Internet to learn about a hobby rather than to seek out new friendships. Studies show that offline friend contact was negatively correlated with online communication, suggesting it replaced rather than contributed to friendship-making skills. Second, and more important, is that the Internet is not a safe place, as we highlight in Chapter Eleven. For this reason, the PEERS program teaches to use the Internet only to contact people already known offline rather than to make new friends and only to arrange in-person contacts. Chapters Four through Seven in this book present ways to overcome communication deficits.

Appropriate Friends for Teens on the Spectrum

Who should the teen on the spectrum try to befriend: Other teens with disabilities or neurotypical teens? The current political climate favors full inclusion. Does this mean full inclusion in the friendships of neurotypical teens? What might the teens themselves want? What turns out better for them? These are questions we seek to answer in this chapter. Full inclusion not only exposes teens on the spectrum to neurotypical teens but also to other teens on the spectrum who are at their social level and may better understand them and overlook their eccentricities.

There is most certainly a split in terms of the benefits of fostering friend-ships with neurotypical teens that cuts along lines of social and verbal skills, especially receptive language ability. Students with lower skills, such as those in special education who are not fully included, may benefit more from associating with others who are on the spectrum or also have disabilities. In this case, when both friends have disabilities, friendships are more sta-ble and companionate than friendships between teens with developmental disabilities and neurotypical peers. The most stable friendships are between students with a long history together—those who went through the same special education classes together, sometimes for many years. This fits with these kids' own desire for more enduring friendships.

Higher-functioning teens on the spectrum seek out friendships with neurotypical teens. They desire to be friends with neurotypical teens not because they form a stronger emotional bond with these teens but because they feel more a part of the mainstream. Friendships of these kids on the spectrum with higher verbal and social skills were found to be more durable and to exhibit higher levels of goal-oriented social behaviors and positive affect. They seemed to have more fun together and appeared closer to each other than when they are friends with other students with disabilities.

Much of what we know about the get-togethers of students on the spec-trum comes from research on preteens or preteens mixed together with teens on the spectrum. The teens under study have not had the benefit of effective social skills training of friendships skills. Observations of get-togethers with other students with disabilities (most likely also on the spectrum) were con-trasted with get-togethers with neurotypical teens. Comparisons of mothers' reports of teens on the spectrum who had neurotypical friends with those of teens who had friends with disabilities suggest that the friendships are just as durable, the friends were usually of the same sex and similar ages, and the parents played a substantial role in getting the friends together and supervising the get-togethers.

Mothers' reports of activities on get-togethers suggest substantial dif-ferences in terms of quality of get-togethers. The most frequently reported activities engaged in with a neurotypical friend was watching videos and TV together (71.4 percent), followed by computer activities (57.2 percent). In contrast, when the invited guest also had a disability, the most common activity was board games (85.7 percent) and talking together (42.8 percent). These differences suggest that teens on the spectrum were more comfortable engaging with other teens with disabilities and could potentially develop a deeper friendship with them than with neurotypical teens. There clearly were individual differences, and best approaches must be decided on an individual basis. Nevertheless, these results suggest that even when a teen would prefer a neurotypical friend, they may have a closer friendship with another teen with disabilities.

Lower-quality friendships would be an issue when either or both teens did not have the benefits of evidence-based social skill training. School-based programs are probably the best venue to accomplish this since both friends are likely to first meet at school and then go on to be better friends and both friends could have social skills training.

Clearly there is a role for both types of friendships. Friendships with neurotypical peers may be more superficial but make the teen feel part of the mainstream. Friendships with other teens on the spectrum may involve more mutual acceptance and understanding. Social skills interventions in the school have the great advantage of providing teens on the spectrum with potential friends from among other teens on the spectrum who are also socially skilled (or will be after evidence-based social skills training).

Common Errors Adults Make in Offering Friendship Help

Well-meaning adults typically make three kinds of errors in trying to help students on the spectrum with their social problems.

Requiring Inclusion

The first is to require inclusion. This is more common in elementary school, where a typical approach is to prohibit students from turning down anyone wishing to join a game. In middle and high schools, this is usually stated as a school policy against ostracism and related to the school antibullying program. We review the prohibition against ostracism in detail in Chapter Eleven. These types of policies are reasonable when referring to including everyone in a group that is assigned to work together on a class project. As mentioned in Chapter Eleven, using the threat of ostracism as a technique to control another student's behavior is never acceptable.

Friendship, however, is a choice. Requiring students to be friends with everyone overlooks the social fabric of our society. Making neurotypical teens feel bad if they don't include a teen on the spectrum in their personal interactions is not going to help teens on the spectrum in the long run. It's a mistake for two reasons to ask neurotypical adolescents to be friends with the teen with autism spectrum disorders. First, it is not consistent with friendship formation to ask someone to be friends for altruistic reasons. Asking neurotypical teens to befriend the teen on the spectrum would be asking them to behave unnaturally. They couldn't be genuine friends. Friendship is a mutual choice, in part based on commonalities in interests, mutual regard, and liking. Second, telling others to be friends with the teen on the spectrum doesn't allow him to learn to make his own friends. It fails to acknowledge his autonomy and is disabling rather than enabling.

Attempting to Pair Students

The second error that well-meaning adults make in trying to help the social integration of kids on the spectrum is matchmaking, where an adult attempts to pair together teens they think should be friends. Usually the students involved are not consulted in adequate detail before arranging the first meeting. Thus, it's not clear at the outset if this match is completely mutual. Nor is it clear that the match is based on qualities that are important to either teen. Third, it doesn't allow kids to learn how to find friends themselves.

Assigning Peer Buddies

The third error that is frequently made is in assigning a neurotypical student as a peer buddy to a teen on the spectrum. The role of the peer buddy is often poorly defined, and the neurotypical peer buddy has received little or no training to help understand the challenges facing the teen on the spectrum and how best to help. Frequently the situation is set up so that boundaries are murky between this peer buddy role and that of a true friend. The relationship between the peer buddy and the teen on the spectrum is unlikely to transcend the school situation, unlikely to last, and unlikely to have the mutuality of a true friendship. Chapter Twelve reviews how to set up a peer mentorship as an effective way of helping teens on the spectrum.

How Educators Can Help Foster Friendships of Teens on the Spectrum

Clearly some teens on the spectrum can maintain friendships with neurotypical teens quite well. (About half the teens on the spectrum in our three-year follow-up study were able to do this after PEERS or Children's Friendship Training.) Some are adolescents desirous of these friendships but lack the verbal skills necessary to form mutually satisfying relationships. Others are perhaps happier because they more easily fit in with others on the spectrum and form lasting friendships. We believe that the lower-quality friendships reported when both friends are on the spectrum stem from the fact that one or both students lack adequate social skills. Teachers are in an ideal position to rectify this by teaching all of the tweens and teens on the spectrum in a school to have better skills and thus improving the relationships among teens on the spectrum.

Chapter Two reviewed strategies that are successful with students with disabilities who successfully integrated themselves into the peer group. One striking adjustment was that they were cautious in their friendly approaches to their neurotypical peers, and this has been the philosophy guiding our interventions. Teens with autism spectrum disorder should be cautious in their approaches to other teens for numerous reasons. Teachers can help teens maintain this caution and help them selectively meet potential friends.

The first question to ask is how strong the desire for friendship is in the teen. If the teen doesn't appear to have a high level of social interest and social activity—for instance, he is quite happy staying home and watching daytime serials on TV—then perhaps he is not ready to have friends. Potential friends should have some shared interests so that they easily find activities to do together. If they have narrow interests but want to fit in, then the lesson plan of Chapter Four will help with this.

The next focus should be on thinking about where the teen fits into the social fabric of the school. As we noted in Chapter Two, the crowd is very important in the process of defining teen identity. And as our experiences with the PEERS intervention have shown us, this social feature is important to consider. If the teacher thinks that a teen on the spectrum might have interests, activities, and social skills adequate to fit into one of the neurotypical crowds, the search should start for other kids in the crowd who may like to get together with the teen on the spectrum.

The qualities of potential friends are different depending on whether the most appropriate potential friend is also on the spectrum or is neurotypical. If a potential friend on the spectrum is more appropriate, then he should have a similar level of overall functioning, social expressiveness, and sensitivity. If the potential friend is a neurotypical teen, he should be open, responsive, and warm—qualities expected of any friend. Either type of friend should live close enough to the teen in question so that it is practicable for parents of both teens to transport them or, if they are old enough and able, to easily get to each other on their own.

Once teachers have identified potential pairs who share common areas of interest or demonstrate mutual interest in one another, they could arrange to have them work together on a shared project to see how they get along. If everything works well, the next step is to inform the parents of both teens of a possible budding friendship. Have the parents first ask the teens if they are interested in getting together. If both are interested, then have one parent talk to the other in order to arrange get-togethers outside of school.

HINTS FOR TEACHERS TO HELP ADOLESCENTS ON THE AUTISM SPECTRUM FIND CLOSE FRIENDS

- Important qualities of friends that students with disabilities report were (in order of frequency of reports) that they did things with each other, saw them in more than one location, shared interests with their friends, and were friends for a long time.
- Many teens on the spectrum may have to learn to fit in with a suitable crowd. (See Chapter Two.)
- Friendships with neurotypical peers may be more superficial but make the adolescent feel part of the mainstream. Friendships with other teens on the spectrum may have more mutual acceptance and understanding.
- Only some tweens and teens on the spectrum will be able to maintain friendships with neurotypical peers.

- The Internet should be avoided as a source of friends. (See Chapter Eleven.)
- Do not require neurotypical teens to be friends with teens on the spectrum.
- First assess how much the teen wants friends. Next assess if he has interests wide enough to maintain friendships (see Chapter Four). Then identify the crowd the teen might best fit into.
- Once you have identified a potential pair who shares common areas of interest or demonstrates mutual interest in one another, arrange to have them work together on a shared project to see if there is chemistry between them.
- Alert the parents of these students if this seems to be a good match.

PART THREE

MORE INTENSIVE INTERVENTIONS TO HELP KIDS FIT IN

CHAPTER 9

Understanding and Assessing Anxiety

" *A student in a language arts class in middle school was asked to share his freewriting assignment with the teacher and one other peer in a small group conversation. This exercise was designed to promote an exchange of ideas, constructive feedback, and practice with verbalizing remarks about written work in a safe learning situation. The student crossed his arms, averted eye gaze from both the teacher and the peer, and angrily looked down. He spoke extremely softly with one- or two-word responses to the teacher's requests to share his ideas. The peer good-naturedly attempted to do his part in the small group discussion, but this did not reduce the resistance of the student on the spectrum at all. After ten minutes of failing to engage this student, the teacher sent the two students back to their desks.* "

Many educators are surprised to learn that anxiety disorders are common in teens with autism spectrum disorders. Approximately 50 to 75 percent of teens with an autism spectrum disorder also have an anxiety disorder, and higher-functioning kids on the spectrum are more likely to have an anxiety disorder than lower-functioning kids. This anxiety exacerbates the adjustment problems that these teens already experience as a result of their autism. Because the experience of anxiety is somewhat private and teens on the spectrum don't communicate their anxiety, others may not be aware of a teen's anxiety level. This chapter focuses on understanding what anxiety is, how it affects teens on the spectrum, and identifying types of anxiety disorders. The next chapter presents lesson plans that can help students cope.

How Anxiety Works

Most people experience some anxiety on a regular basis, so much so that it seems to be a basic part of life. Studies show that moderate levels of anxiety help people increase their level of effort when they are working on important tasks. Consider the anxiety that we've all experienced when studying for an important test in high school or college, one that has a potential impact on our future educational and occupational options. The anxiety we get from thinking about our larger goals causes us to increase our focus: we put aside anything that might otherwise seem more interesting and distract our attention, like television, and increase our attention to the source of our anxiety.

Irrational concerns may also trigger anxiety. For example, the slight anxiety we feel when standing in front of a large plate glass window at the top of a high building is triggered by our subconscious perception of the possibility that we might fall. Although it is an unpleasant and often suppressed thought, our demise is the central concern that triggers a physical sense of tension and anxiety—a precursor of the fight-or-flight reflex—even in the face of evidence that the window in front of us is keeping us safe.

Feelings of anxiety, worry, and fear occur when we focus on our perceptions of danger. These emotions occur in advance of events that might be threatening but won't necessarily occur. As the threat seems to be closer at hand and becomes more likely and more severe, we move from slightly bothersome worried thoughts to moderately consuming anxiety, to all-out dread, fear, and even panic. For example, a common type of anxiety that most of us have experienced is public speaking anxiety. When a feared upcoming speech is still far in the future, it is common to think how unpleasant it might be and all of the things that could go wrong. As the day, and then the hour, approaches, tension, shivering, nausea, and a desire to avoid the speech may build to almost intolerable proportions.

Anxiety begins in the brain when we notice or think of something threatening. A chemical message is then sent to the limbic system area of the brain, which initiates a release of hormones, including adrenaline, which flows throughout the body in the bloodstream. The adrenaline triggers muscular tension, sweating, sometimes a sense of nausea, and at high levels of adrenaline, even vomiting. This adrenaline rush helps us escape from serious threats by increasing muscle tone and maximizing our capacity to act in self-defense. However, this activation is often out of proportion to the kinds of threats that people experience in everyday life. These stresses are often merely nuisances or frustrations rather than existential threats. Nevertheless, our brains are wired to react in the same way whether we are truly in danger or merely nervous about a social situation outside our comfort zone. The fight-or-flight reflex set off by this adrenaline rush leads to diminished attention toward anything other than the perceived danger, even if the danger seems trivial to others, such as answering a question in class or working in a small group with peers.

Anxiety can cause unpleasant physical sensations such as tension, negative mood (many teens on the spectrum report feeling "bad," "uncomfortable," or "cranky," for example), and fearful thoughts about future events. These sensations and worries gradually disappear once the perceived danger passes, leading to a sense of relief that often gives teens the impression that there was something to be truly afraid of ("I feel so much better now that I don't have to worry anymore"). The fight-or-flight reflex comes with high levels of anxiety. When a danger seems imminent and anxiety begins to peak, the natural tendency is to avoid the situation at all costs or, if that fails, to become hostile and explosive (or sometimes to retreat and find a safe place to hide).

Clinical Levels of Anxiety

People with chronic, irrational anxiety tend to feel uncomfortable and threatened in unfamiliar or ambiguous situations much more than others do. This is because they are more prone to have fight-or-flight reactions triggered by trivial events. They have a "loose trigger" reaction style that activates an adrenaline rush with relatively little provocation. This leads to many false alarms as people with this type of reaction style often get nervous and wound up over issues that are manageable or inconsequential for most other people.

Clinical levels of anxiety may also be a gateway to depression, which can have particularly serious consequences in the long and short terms. Feeling a constant sense of threat and danger appears to leave many adolescents feeling hopeless and inadequate. These perceptions are precursors of clinical depression, a condition that may lead to troubling behaviors such as suicidal thinking and can be difficult to treat. Numerous studies have found that, as with anxiety problems, tweens and teens on the spectrum are more susceptible to depression and suicidality than are neurotypical kids. For many adolescents, anxiety and depression can trigger substance abuse problems. Although there is less research on substance abuse in teens on the spectrum, some studies suggest that substance use disorders are relatively common among adults with autism. Much of the substance abuse that occurs in teens are attempts at self-medication to reduce anxiety and depression. While substance abuse temporarily results in relief from negative feelings, it quickly can develop into its own clinical problem with impulsive, erratic, and sometimes dangerous behaviors as well as dependence. Some studies with neurotypical adolescents have found that by intervening effectively with anxiety, depression and substance abuse can be prevented or reduced in severity.

How Anxiety Exacerbates Symptoms of Autism Spectrum Disorder

Teens on the spectrum often experience a high level of anxiety that becomes so distracting that it takes a further toll on social life and academic performance. Jeffrey Wood's research has shown that increases in anxiety over the course of a year tend to lead teens to reduced academic success, reduced social adjustment with peers, and increased absence from school.

Stressful daily events for students on the spectrum are common and increase anxiety and negative mood. The sources of stress include:

- The stress of social confusion and the result of failing to meet one's social goals on a recurrent basis

- The stress of being prevented from accessing preferred activities and special interests in settings such as school and home

- The stress of peer rejection and victimization that most adolescents on the spectrum experience

- Sensitivities to sound, light, and touch that many individuals on the spectrum experience

These autism-specific stressful events that many young people on the spectrum experience routinely prime their brains to be in a constant state of readiness for the fight-or-flight reflex. This puts them on edge, reduces their comfort, and makes them prone to perceive the world more negatively. In this chronically distressed state, anxiety and other disorders of negative emotion are more likely to arise, particularly for those who are already genetically predisposed to mood disorders.

Adolescents with severe anxiety are incapable of distinguishing between realistic threats and catastrophic events that are unlikely to happen. They tend to misinterpret the feedback that they receive as negative and punishing. For instance, teens with high social anxiety commonly misinterpret neutral reactions to a class presentation as a form of rejection or even hostility toward them. One tenth-grader with low-average mental ability was preoccupied with upcoming presentations that were a core element of the curriculum in his primarily mainstream classes. At home, he frequently spoke of how other students thought he was "an idiot or loser." He emphasized the way that peers looked at him during his presentations. Teachers reported that the students often had a bored and glazed-over look during many presentations, including his, and that they had seen no signs of mocking or derision directed toward this boy. Nonetheless, he was convinced of his more negative interpretation, a perception that reduced his confidence about participating in social events with his peers. He would insist that he was not liked and not welcome.

Many teens on the spectrum are anxious about being anxious. They are reluctant to speak about their social anxiety and feel embarrassed about it. Instead they often give excuses for not participating, such as, "I don't like that topic," or, "I don't know how to do it," or, "That's not my interest." However, to trusted adults, the real explanation is often much more anxiety based—for example, "The other kids wouldn't like me," or, "They'll think I've got a dumb voice," or, "Everyone will laugh at me." A high school student on the spectrum was asked to play a role in a new school play. He had enjoyed acting in earlier years and had had some theatrical success. As a structured activity, it offered him a chance to get to know some other teens doing something he had competence in—an ideal circumstance for building relationships. Nonetheless, he declined, saying that he wasn't really interested in acting anymore. In private, he told his therapist that he had "wimped out" because he felt intimidated by a group of popular teens who "always were in the school plays," and he felt that they would never accept him. After the fact, however, he acknowledged that there were also a number of teens in the play who weren't especially popular whom he wished he had had the chance to get to know. For teens with some insight, the experience of irrational social anxiety is accompanied by regret over lost social opportunities.

Another example is the teen on the spectrum who was asked by a peer why he always stayed in the library by himself during lunch. He gave the excuse that he was too busy doing chores at home to get any homework done there, so he did it during lunchtime. In fact, he had no self-confidence about joining any of the groups at lunch.

Failure to participate in class due to shyness or to attend school or remain in class for the full class period are other examples of the effects of social anxiety in teens on the spectrum. In general, any all-consuming worry is likely to reduce attention to the here-and-now and interfere with social bonding and academic focus. For example, one thirteen-year-old boy on the spectrum was preoccupied with his mother's safety when he was away from her. In the first several weeks of eighth grade, he seemed nervous and preoccupied to his teachers and not mentally present in class. Then he began missing school on an increasingly frequent basis with complaints of nausea and headaches. Multiple doctor appointments could establish no medical basis for the complaints. Yet the boy got into a pattern of chronic school absence due to his physical complaints. An anxiety assessment revealed the underlying fears causing his physical symptoms. Unfortunately, by the time an intervention was mounted, the boy had missed several months of school and felt left behind by his peers' conversations and activities.

Outbursts and Meltdowns

Perhaps the most puzzling behaviors of teens on the spectrum who are in regular education classes are the meltdowns—that is, outbursts of yelling, crying, or resistance that are sustained for several minutes or longer. Many of these meltdowns are related to anxiety problems and not willfulness, oppositional behavior, or defiance. Consider a student who was increasingly stressed out on a particular day by the amount of noise in his classroom. This stress led to increasing thoughts of victimization and a lack of control, and he eventually blurted out at the top of his lungs, "Will you all please stop torturing me? I can't take this noise pollution you're creating for one more second!" He then dissolved into tears and wails. He resisted his teacher's efforts to escort him to a more private place, telling her, "Don't touch me. Leave me alone."

The student later described to his teacher his increasing fearfulness of "losing his mind" in reaction to the noisy classroom. Although a variety of responses on his part could have led to a reduction of this noise in a more productive manner (he could have asked to be excused to go to a quieter place or explained that he was on the verge on losing his temper, for example), his anxiety propelled the outburst in front of the class in an automatic, unplanned way. This is characteristic of the fight-or-flight reflex. Such outbursts can have significant consequences for a teen's peer relationships as well as the student–teacher relationship.

Another example is the teen on the spectrum who was cornered into doing things he feared. He would have loud, threatening outbursts when called on in class if he felt uncertain about the answer or thought the teacher was trying to embarrass him. It is important to recognize that in spite of the uncontrolled, disorganized, and hostile quality of this teen's behavior, this behavior was the end point of a buildup of anxiety that he did not manage effectively.

Students on the spectrum already have plenty to manage as a result of their disorder. The additional burden of anxiety can at times paralyze their progress in social and academic competence.

Types of Anxiety in Students with Autism

In addition to general anxiety reactions, there are three main types of specific anxiety disorders identified by the American Psychological Association's *Diagnostic and Statistical Manual of Mental Disorders*: social anxiety, generalized anxiety, and separation anxiety. Teens on the autism spectrum are likely to have any of these.

Social Anxiety

Because high-functioning teens with autism spectrum disorders want to be accepted by their peers and realize that they fall short, they are more likely than not to have social anxiety. Their primary social anxieties center on the concern that they will be embarrassed or humiliated in specific social settings, and so they are apprehensive about or resistant to engaging socially. The following forms of social anxiety for teens on the autism spectrum are especially common:

- A reluctance to interact with peers during class projects
- Avoidance of asking for help from teachers
- A tendency not to want to participate in class discussions
- A failure to volunteer answers
- A very quiet voice or a meek and timid way of speaking
- An unengaged and shrinking emotional reaction to one-on-one discussions with the teacher

The focus of social anxiety can be far-reaching and can include discomfort in specific social situations such as eating in front of others, using public bathrooms, going to parties, saying no to others' bad ideas, nonverbal performances like writing on the board or playing an instrument in front of a group, and, of course, public speaking.

Anxiety can be magnified in several ways during public speaking. All attention seems to be on the speaker, making it difficult to mask a mistake; moreover, multiple people are observing, resulting in a potential topic of gossip and critical rumors that could, in theory, be hard to live down and overcome. It's because the stakes seem so high that many adolescents fall victim to public speaking anxiety. This is especially true for kids on the spectrum who already find communication and social interactions challenging, even in one-to-one situations.

Social anxiety among kids on the spectrum often has its roots in years of social confusion, social mishaps, and rejection or isolation. Even when they master new social skills or conditions change and peers become more receptive to the affected teen, this social anxiety can continue to dominate the teen's social style and willingness to try to socially engage. One teen girl on the spectrum had become highly motivated to form relationships with peers as she entered middle school after years of relative indifference about friendships. She was unwilling to act on this interest, however, because she was paralyzed by worry about the consequences of initiating social interactions, such as rejection, gossip, and bullying. Anxious avoidance of interactions is a common outcome for a teen with these concerns, and it is the product of an unfortunate paradox. The social motivation that often arises in higher-functioning teens on the spectrum brings with it a realization of the difficulty of fitting in and finding a friend or group. Once these teens decide that they want friendships, their low self-confidence and anxiety about social failure frequently handcuff them, even after they are taught appropriate approach skills, perpetuating their social isolation.

At the beginning of this chapter, we described a student who was reserved and avoidant during a structured small group conversation with one classmate and his teacher. After the students returned to their desks, the teacher offered to discuss the experience. The student said that he felt confused about effectively summarizing his written work without simply reading it verbatim to his peer. With structured discussion, using the anxiety management techniques presented in the lesson plans in Chapter Ten, he revealed that he feared that he would humiliate himself with unintelligible remarks. This was a common pattern for him. When he was asked to participate in activities involving speaking in class, he became defiant and hostile. Typically he would have very little to say. Strikingly, the teacher had observed the same student regularly enjoy chitchat about video games and other interests with several others in the class. She was confused by the fact that the student seemed to have the communication abilities necessary for small group discussions yet was consistently defiant. She felt that general teaching strategies such as assigning modified versions of the task and giving him encouragement had not helped him make progress in this area.

When social anxiety is overwhelming, anxiety symptoms can inhibit performance in social situations in which a teen has to engage. Symptoms such as verbal dysfluency, pausing, stuttering, and word-finding problems are common. At the extreme, symptoms of anxiety can take the form of selective mutism: never speaking in class, never speaking in school, or speaking only in a very quiet voice or only to peers under select conditions. One fourteen-year-old boy on the spectrum with average intelligence and oral language abilities had an odd mannerism with his hands that he found hard to control, and he was so embarrassed by it that he had developed a strategy of bringing as little attention to himself as possible by speaking only rarely at school. He would whisper when teachers initiated a conversation, but he never participated in class discussions and rarely spoke to his classmates. Nonetheless, in comfortable settings at home, he could be talkative and funny. His anxiety greatly impaired his social skills.

Adolescents with high social anxiety lack insight into the irrationality of their fears of the consequences of social participation. A common fear is that any attempt they make to participate will lead to permanent rejection and ridicule by peers. Unfortunately, there is a paradox: when irrational fears dominate a teen's thoughts, it is especially difficult for them to act casual and socially competent, increasing the chances that their fears of rejection could be realized.

Generalized Anxiety

In contrast to social anxiety, generalized anxiety is focused on potential dangers in multiple aspects of life: school performance, home life, and problems in society, health, and others areas. Generalized anxiety is characterized primarily by worry, the cognitive or thought-based component of anxiety. Generalized anxiety is typified by many different worries, with an irrational sense of threat and adverse consequences. Worries can always be put into words and are what we dwell on when we anticipate future problems. When we get stuck in traffic and repeat to ourselves, "I can't be late, I have all this prep to do before class and it'll be a disaster if it's not ready," this is worry. Excessive worry can affect a teen's experiences with peers, often making them blow things out of proportion. For example, if a friend made a rude remark to a teen, the teen might catastrophize with thoughts such as, "She seems to hate me all of a sudden, and my social life is going straight down the tank," or even, "Since she is rejecting me, I may as well give up on ever having a decent social life. She was the only person who wanted to be my friend, and now she hates me too." A more reasonable reaction might be, "I wonder if she is having a bad day today?" or perhaps, "Was it something I did wrong?" Problems can certainly occur in life, but many of them are fixable; generalized anxiety, however, tends to make teens feel that everyday problems are the end of the world.

Other symptoms of generalized anxiety for kids on the spectrum include worries about performance in school and homework and extracurricular activities, one's personal appearance or peer group dynamics such as gossip, world events such as war and crime or the environment, community issues such as homelessness, and one's health or a parent's health. Teens rarely experience disturbing worries in all of these areas, but because of the pervasive nature of generalized anxiety disorder, multiple worries that are distracting, upsetting, and sometimes consuming are common in affected adolescents.

It is often surprising to teachers (and parents) that some teens on the spectrum experience some of these concerns—for example, about personal appearance. Common reports by parents and teachers suggest that teens on the spectrum can be oblivious about their appearance. However, it is worth remembering two things. First, the autism spectrum is wide and includes teens with varying patterns of strengths and weaknesses. We regularly see higher-functioning teens with excessive worry that they don't have "perfect-looking hair," feel hypersensitive that small stains on their clothing will cause them to stand out, or complain that their wardrobe is suddenly out-of-fashion and embarrassing. These worries are often inaccurate in terms of the actual consequences, but teens on the spectrum (and some neurotypical teens as well) feel these acutely in spite of the lack of evidence.

Generalized anxieties can be relatively easy to miss for adults who work with students on the spectrum. There are ways that these anxieties can emerge that do not necessarily sound like clinical symptoms, but nonetheless give some indication of the teen's area of concern. For instance, knowledge of certain topics in great detail that are unexpected for the teen's age can be a tip-off. As one example, a student on the spectrum had uncommon knowledge of nuclear weapons, including weapon categories and arsenals of the various nuclear weapons states. This boy secretly had an excessive worry and preoccupation with the threat of nuclear war.

Separation Anxiety

Another frequent and problematic anxiety in teens on the autism spectrum is separation anxiety. Affected teens are often troubled by a belief that they or their caregivers are in danger when they're apart from each other. Concerns about kidnappers, thieves, car accidents, natural disasters, terrorism, a sudden breakout of war, and other rare incidents are common foundational worries for this aspect of anxiety in teens. In general, their irrational belief is that by being apart from parents, they are in great danger because they believe their parents could protect them from these kinds of happenings. Therefore, adolescents on the spectrum with high separation anxiety are reluctant to be away from their parents. Separation anxiety is rooted in primitive early childhood bonding that typically promotes safety among the young of many species. This basic instinct, which is also thought to promote feelings of attachment and love, can become distorted by irrational anxiety and turned into unnecessary worry. As with all other anxiety disorders affecting teens on the spectrum, the fears are irrational.

Signs of separation anxiety in teenagers on the spectrum include reluctance to attend school, frequent absences, frequent visits to the nurse's office in an attempt to contact parents or have school personnel check in with parents on the student's behalf, and frequent unnecessary cell phone calls to parents throughout the day. Recently one of us (Jeffrey) worked with school nurses to identify students for intervention because the nurses were well aware of the anxiety driving certain students' repeated visits.

Some students with this anxiety go to great lengths to avoid separations, including acting-out behavior that others often misinterpret as defiance or aggression. On school days, parents report yelling, hitting, defiant comments, and even reckless behaviors such as opening the car door—during the drive to school. Such behaviors can occur at home, on the way to school, or at drop-off. A teen with separation anxiety who is compelled to go to school anyway may be easily triggered into a tantrum within the first hour or two of the school day.

In some more extreme cases of school-related separation anxiety, teens have been known to experience panic attacks at home before the school day begins, vomiting, lying on the floor of their bathroom, and clinging to furniture as parents attempt to physically escort the teen to the door. These unfortunate confrontations are distressing for all and exemplify the level of panic experienced by teens who often perceive such separations as having life-and-death implications.

One effective means of reducing separation anxiety in some cases is to help adolescents recognize when the odds of a feared outcome, say, kidnapping, are exceptionally low (perhaps 1 out of 1 million) for where they live. This and other techniques are discussed extensively in the anxiety lesson plans in Chapter Ten. An important initial approach for educators is to give little attention and make few demands until the teen is visibly calmer. In spite of the aggressive and impulsive qualities of these behaviors, they are best understood as an expression of primitive fear about abandonment and threat to the self or to loved ones. Thus, when these behaviors occur in reaction to separations, the anxiety intervention in the lesson plans in Chapter Ten is much more suitable and likely to work than school-based punishments or suspensions.

Assessing Anxiety

Assessing anxiety problems in students on the spectrum serves two main functions. The first is to determine whether a significant anxiety may be playing a role in a student's social and academic adjustment problems. The second is to identify specific symptoms of anxiety that may benefit from focused intervention techniques. While assessments of symptoms of fear and worry are important, the assessment of meltdowns and other anxiety-related behavior problems is equally important in determining whether an anxiety intervention may be beneficial.

Anxiety can escape the attention of parents, teachers, and mental health practitioners. As a result, many teens in school and clinical settings have undetected anxiety unless they are screened for it. A challenge of screening teens on the spectrum for anxiety is that while anxiety is in part a private experience, one of the characteristics of the autism spectrum is reduced awareness and ability to describe a range of emotions. The jury is still out on how accurately teens on the spectrum can self-report on their anxiety. However, preliminary research, including studies that Jeffrey Wood has conducted in the past several years, have suggested that parents, teachers, and the teens themselves can each offer a unique perspective with some validity.

Parents and teachers are each uniquely able to observe the symptoms of anxiety in teens on the spectrum: worried remarks about specific social situations, fearful avoidance of certain social situations, word-finding problems and alterations of speech patterns (such as a very quiet voice) in anxious situations relative to a teen's typical speech, and increased rigidity and perfectionism when the teen is concerned with performance. An example of the last symptom is a seventh grader on the spectrum who appeared mostly easygoing during class, but became oppositional and defiant when confronted with any kind of written class work. The student maintained that she could not do the work in spite of evidence to the contrary (for example, she had completed written homework). This pattern may appear to reflect a simple reluctance to engage in hard work. For many students on the spectrum with high anxiety, it indicates a perfectionistic work standard that paradoxically leads to freezing or refusal to do the work. This paradox reflects the maladaptive coping strategy of avoidance: some students with anxiety prefer to look lazy or uninterested rather than take the risk of achieving anything less than complete success.

Teachers are in a unique place to judge anxiety in teens on the spectrum. By virtue of their extensive contact with their students, they can quickly and accurately assess anxiety symptoms. In our research, we have found six especially useful signs of anxiety that teachers can use as a short screening for anxiety:

- Being unduly afraid that other kids will laugh or make fun of him or her

- Having worries about being called on in class

- Exhibiting worries about what other people seem to think of him or her

- Trying to do everything exactly right or showing other signs of perfectionism

- Showing excessive worry about performance in school or being hypersensitive to criticism

- Having difficulty separating from parents before school or showing preoccupation about parents' whereabouts and issues such as whether a parent will be on time to pick up the teen from school or repeatedly trying to phone the parent in the middle of the school day

Students who frequently miss school or visit the school nurse more than appears necessary also often are showing signs of the avoidant aspects of anxiety. Symptoms of school and class avoidance are not always anxiety related. For example, some teenagers appear to use such avoidance to deal with a poor attention span, low interest, learning difficulties, or avoiding being victimized. In general, the more symptoms of anxiety, the more probable that a young person has a significant anxiety problem.

Three questions can help determine whether meltdowns and other behavior problems may be anxiety related:

1. Does the student exhibit rigidity, defiance, or outbursts when confronted with situations that make him or her feel unconfident or perfectionistic?

2. Does social attention toward the student sometimes result in hostility, reduced participation, and quiet defiance?

3. Are sensory issues, confusion, or embarrassment causing anxiety and outbursts? Students who experience high levels of stress due to specific

causes such as sensitivity to sound, light, or touch; failure to comprehend instructions or expectations; and perceptions, correct or otherwise, of social slights from peers may feel anxiety and act out in response by shouting, crying, making hostile remarks, and refusing to go along with requests.

More formal questionnaire measures can be helpful in developing a broader assessment of possible anxiety issues for teens on the spectrum. We have developed a related set of three such questionnaires for this purpose: one rated by teachers, one by students, and one by parents (Handouts 9.1 through 9.3). The teacher-report questionnaire can be used as a tool for considering the range of common anxiety symptoms exhibited by teens on the spectrum in classroom settings and rating the frequency or severity of each. This questionnaire covers issues of social, generalized, and separation anxiety, including the possibility of anxiety-related hostility and meltdowns.

To engage the parents of a student on the spectrum in the assessment process and alert them to the possibility of an anxiety intervention, a sample cover letter to parents is included as Handout 9.4. Send this letter home along with the parent anxiety checklist, perhaps in the form of a confidential letter mailed to the parents. This way, the teen will not inadvertently read any material such as the wording of the parent checklist items and feel offended or embarrassed or, conversely, complete the checklist for himself, presumably less accurately than the parents would have completed it, and return it as though the parents had filled it out.

Mental health professionals are often trained to assess for anxiety problems in teenagers. Depending on the circumstances, an evaluation by an expert in teen anxiety disorders may be called for if anxiety appears to be severe or significant enough to warrant clinical attention. Potential referrals may be found through local sources or from the Web site of the professional Association for Behavioral and Cognitive Therapy (www.abct.org). However, there is much that teachers can do for many students on the spectrum without additional support of this kind.

After identifying the key areas of anxiety for the student, whether they are focused primarily on the fear of social humiliation and rejection, experience extensive worry about a variety of topics, or experience feelings of separation anxiety with regard to parents and possibly also with regard to dependency on teachers, you will have a clear idea of the nature of the emotional challenges facing the student and what the intervention should set out to address.

A commonly used free questionnaire measure developed for parent and youth reports (but not teachers) is the SCARED checklist. Teachers can access this resource online (teen version: http://www.wpic.pitt.edu/research/AssessmentTools/ChildAdolescent/ScaredChild-final.pdf; parent version: http://www.wpic.pitt.edu/research/AssessmentTools/ChildAdolescent/ScaredParent-final.pdf). The scores generated by this questionnaire can be compared with a clinical cutoff score to give teachers and other school professionals a sense of the severity of a teen's anxiety symptoms. Give either the questionnaires in Handouts 9.1 through 9.3 or just the SCARED to teens and parents.

HANDOUT 9.1 Teacher's Anxiety Questionnaire for Students with Autism Spectrum Disorders

Indicate how frequently your student exhibits the following anxiety issues. If you are unsure of an item, make your best assessment. Don't spend too much time on any particular item.

Scoring: Assign the following points to each answer: never = 0, rarely = 1, sometimes = 2, and often = 3. Total scores greater than 10 indicate significant anxiety symptoms.

		NEVER	RARELY	SOMETIMES	OFTEN
1.	My student seems physically panicked.				
2.	My student worries about his or her health.				
3.	My student tries to stay close to where I am.				
4.	My student trembles visibly.				
5.	My student seems to worry about social issues like homelessness.				
6.	My student seems embarrassed in front of others.				
7.	My student seems clingy to me.				
8.	My student complains of headache or stomachache.				
9.	My student seems to worry about the environment, the economy, politics, equality, and other similar topics.				
10.	My student is scared of saying the wrong thing.				
11.	My student is easily startled.				
12.	My student blushes easily.				
13.	My student worries about minor social happenings in his or her peer group.				
14.	My student worries that no one will like him or her.				
15.	My student seems overly attached to me for his or her age.				
16.	My student overreacts when surprised.				

		NEVER	RARELY	SOMETIMES	OFTEN
17.	My student seems to worry about not doing things perfectly.				
18.	My student needs one to stay near him or her at bedtime.				
19.	My student acts stressed out and edgy.				
20.	My student is hard on himself or herself for the slightest things.				
21.	My student is preoccupied with saying the wrong thing around other students.				
22.	My student worries excessively about homework and assignments.				
23.	My student gets quiet and shy when the attention focuses on him or her.				
24.	My student refuses to attend school events that aren't required.				
25.	My student worries about doing well on classwork and tests to the point of distracting himself or herself.				
26.	My student feels people don't want to talk with him or her.				
27.	My student is so perfectionistic that minor failures can lead to meltdowns and outbursts.				
28.	My student seems hostile and angry when social attention is focused on him or her.				
29.	My student's sensitivities to sound and touch lead to outbursts and meltdowns.				
30.	My student's worrying is out of proportion with the issues that bother him or her.				

Total score: _____

Social Skills Success for Students with Autism/Asperger's, copyright © 2011 John Wiley and Sons, Inc.

HANDOUT 9.2 Parents' Anxiety Questionnaire for Adolescents with Autism

Indicate how frequently your child is bothered by the following anxiety issues. If you are unsure of an item, make your best guess. Feel free to jot down notes to clarify your responses. Of course, there are no right or wrong answers; your responses will just give us an idea of how things are going for your child at this time. Don't spend too much time on any particular item.

Scoring: Assign the following points to each answer: never = 0, rarely = 1, sometimes = 2, and often = 3. Total scores greater than 10 indicate significant anxiety symptoms.

		NEVER	RARELY	SOMETIMES	OFTEN
1.	My child feels physical discomfort.				
2.	My child worries about world events like war.				
3.	My child fears others are rejecting him or her.				
4.	My child worries about things happening to me.				
5.	My child seems physically panicked.				
6.	My child worries about his or her health.				
7.	My child tries to stay close to where I am.				
8.	My child trembles visibly.				
9.	My child worries about social issues like homelessness.				
10.	My child is embarrassed in front of others.				
11.	My child avoids separating from me.				
12.	My child complains of headaches or stomachaches.				
13.	My child worries about the environment, the economy, politics, equality, and other similar topics.				
14.	My child is scared of saying the wrong thing.				
15.	My child is easily startled.				

		NEVER	RARELY	SOMETIMES	OFTEN
16.	My child blushes easily.				
17.	My child would still like to sleep in the same room as I do.				
18.	My child complains of nausea and cramps.				
19.	My child is a homebody.				
20.	My child's eyes widen with fear at small things.				
21.	My child worries about the social drama of his or her peer group.				
22.	My child worries that no one will like him or her.				
23.	My child seems overly attached to me for his or her age.				
24.	My child overreacts when surprised.				
25.	My child worries about not doing things perfectly.				
26.	My child needs someone to stay near him or her at bedtime.				
27.	My child acts stressed out and edgy.				
28.	My child is hard on himself or herself for the slightest things.				
29.	My child is preoccupied with saying the wrong thing around other teens.				
30.	My child worries others will think he or she looks weird.				
31.	My child has backaches, neck aches, and shoulder aches that seem to have no physical origin.				
32.	My child worries excessively about homework and assignments.				

Social Skills Success for Students with Autism/Asperger's, copyright © 2011 John Wiley and Sons, Inc.

		NEVER	RARELY	SOMETIMES	OFTEN
33.	My child gets quiet and shy when the attention focuses on him or her.				
34.	My child refuses extracurricular events if they involve being away from me.				
35.	My child worries about doing well on classwork and tests to the point of distracting himself or herself.				
36.	My child checks and rechecks locks, windows, and doors to ensure his or her safety.				
37.	My child feels people would not want to talk with him or her.				
38.	My child is obsessed with washing hands and avoiding contamination.				
39.	My child worries about my health.				
40.	My child gets unpleasant thoughts and images stuck in his or her head.				

Total score: _____

HANDOUT 9.3 Adolescent's Anxiety Questionnaire

Indicate how often you are bothered by the following things. If you are unsure of an answer, make your best guess. There are no right or wrong answers. This will just give us an idea of how things are going for you at this time. Don't spend too much time on any particular question.

Scoring: Assign the following points to each answer: never = 0, rarely = 1, sometimes = 2, and often = 3. Total scores greater than 10 indicate significant anxiety symptoms.

		NEVER	RARELY	SOMETIMES	OFTEN
1.	My body feels uncomfortable.				
2.	I worry about world events like war.				
3.	I fear others are rejecting me.				
4.	I worry about something happening to my parents.				
5.	My body feels freaked out.				
6.	I worry about my health.				
7.	I try to stay close to my parents.				
8.	I tremble on the inside.				
9.	I worry about social issues like homelessness.				
10.	I get embarrassed in front of others.				
11.	I avoid being away from my parents.				
12.	I get headaches and stomachaches.				
13.	I worry about the environment, the economy, politics, and equality.				
14.	I am scared of saying the wrong thing.				
15.	I get startled.				
16.	I blush easily.				
17.	I would still like to sleep in the same room as my parents.				
18.	I get cramps inside my body.				
19.	I am a homebody and don't want to go out.				
20.	My eyes can get wide with fear.				
21.	I worry about the social drama at my school.				

Social Skills Success for Students with Autism/Asperger's, copyright © 2011 John Wiley and Sons Inc

HANDOUT 9.3 (continued)

		NEVER	RARELY	SOMETIMES	OFTEN
22.	I worry that no one will like me.				
23.	I am overly attached to my parents.				
24.	I overreact when I'm surprised.				
25.	I worry about not doing things perfectly.				
26.	I need someone to stay near me when I'm falling asleep.				
27.	I act stressed out and edgy.				
28.	I am hard on myself for the slightest things.				
29.	I am worried about saying the wrong thing around other teens.				
30.	I worry about my clothes and my looks.				
31.	I get backaches, neck aches, or shoulder aches.				
32.	I worry too much about homework and assignments.				
33.	I get quiet and shy when the attention focuses on me.				
34.	I refuse going to after-school events if they involve being away from my parents.				
35.	I worry about doing well on classwork and tests.				
36.	I check and recheck locks, windows, and doors to make sure we're safe.				
37.	I feel people would not want to talk with me.				
38.	I get obsessed with washing hands and avoiding contamination.				
39.	I worry about my parents' health.				
40.	I get unpleasant thoughts and images stuck in my head.				

Total score: _____

HANDOUT 9.4 Letter to Parents

Dear Parent:

Over the next few weeks, we will be working on learning about anxiety and other emotions in our class. Many adolescents have difficulty with managing their emotions and often have a lot of anxieties and fears, as well as other unpleasant emotional experiences. These feelings, while common to everyone at moderate levels, can often get in the way of social adjustment and engagement in class for students on the spectrum.

In order to help determine how anxiety may or may not be playing a role in your child's life currently, I am enclosing an anxiety checklist for you to complete. We had your child complete this checklist in class already, but we would like you to do it as well so that we can get your unique viewpoint about your child's specific areas of anxiety.

When you fill out the form, just make your best guess with regard to which anxieties are current issues for your child. Feel free to write in brief notes on the questionnaire as well if there are particular concerns you may have or specific details you think it would benefit us to know about your child. Please complete this checklist and return it to me by _____.

Thank you for your help with this assessment.

Sincerely,

CHAPTER 10

Interventions to Reduce Anxiety and Outbursts

> *I get this weird feeling like my heart is racing. I feel sick and sometimes get stomachaches and a weak, dizzy feeling in my head. It is hard to stop. If whatever was causing me to become distressed doesn't stop, I go into a rage that I'd only remember parts of. I'm trying to do anything I can to cut off the outside world for a few minutes, while I get my head to reset. People might try to talk to me — which just makes me more verbally forceful in getting away from them.*
>
> *When I started to become more aware of this feeling, I would go into a room by myself, turn the lights off, and put a pillow or towel over my ears so no sound could get in. Then I would just try to 'go numb.' Over time, I became better at it so that I could just close my eyes and go numb. At least this is more socially acceptable.*

Because of the barriers that anxiety can pose to the development of friendship and a student's adjustment at school, anxiety-related interventions are an important tool for teachers working with students on the spectrum in all education settings—both inclusive mainstream and special education settings. Addressing problematic anxiety is rarely a one-shot deal, although much progress can be made in relatively short order if anxiety is circumscribed as opposed to pervasive and ingrained. Teens on the spectrum are more able to focus their attention on successful social and academic strategies when their anxiety is reduced.

According to the results of numerous research studies, cognitive behavioral interventions for anxiety can be effectively delivered by classroom teachers, school psychologists, and school counselors. Studies have shown that teachers are at least as effective as highly trained psychotherapists in administering anxiety-related interventions in a school classroom setting. In planning the intervention, three main delivery approaches work well: training the entire class in anxiety management; training a small group of teens, including the teen on the autism spectrum; and meeting with the teen on the spectrum individually to do the intervention. With the whole class approach, a teacher might set aside five to nine classroom meetings of thirty to sixty minutes each over the course of several weeks or months to teach anxiety management skills to the entire class. The approach has these advantages:

- It doesn't add to the teacher's workload since the intervention is done within regular classroom hours.

- The entire class can benefit from this kind of intervention and show improvements in their own emotion management as well. Research has shown that using anxiety interventions in a preventive manner in classrooms of neurotypical students can lead to the prevention of clinical anxiety and depression in subsequent years for participants who were not selected for any particular emotional problems to begin with.

- The student on the spectrum does not feel singled out. Students on the spectrum can feel relieved to hear that others have similar problems with anxiety and they are not unusual in this regard.

Nonetheless, there are several reasons that teachers may choose other methods of delivering an anxiety-related intervention for teens on the spectrum. Teachers may not have the class time to devote to emotion education, an unfortunate but undeniable aspect of our modern society; they may feel that the program would be too diluted to benefit the student on the spectrum in this format; or the class may not lend itself to such a topic.

An appealing alternative is a small work group of several students, including the student on the autism spectrum. Like a classroom-based presentation format, the small group format has advantages by reducing the student on the spectrum's sense of being different and singled out. Furthermore, the other students are likely to benefit from the intervention as well. Potential times for working with such a group are lunchtime once or twice a week, after school once or twice a week, or before school for twenty- or thirty-minute discussion meetings. In a special education setting, it might also be possible to have a small work group meet with the special education teacher during regular class time while other students are working with a second teacher or aide or are doing independent desk work. The same general considerations also apply to working with students individually. Chapter Three offers some additional tips for running this class.

A key concept for beginning the intervention that is helpful for teachers to recall from Chapter Nine is that irrational anxiety is a false alarm. When an adrenaline rush hits the bloodstream and teens begin feeling tense and having fearful thoughts, they automatically assume that there is a real threat and that some kind of action is necessary to preserve their safety. However, this high anxiety is just a false alarm. Although anxiety is useful in a truly dangerous situation, many other times a fight-or-flight reaction is out of proportion with the threat we confront.

A helpful example of this that teens can understand is when a test is given or a class speech is required, a fight-or-flight reaction may be triggered, to the benefit of no one. The anxiety response is more likely to be a hindrance than a help. The teen might freeze or become distracted with worry and, ironically, not do his best. Although the physical sensations and thoughts of high anxiety are present, such as tension and even nausea, a false alarm has occurred. Having anxious feelings does not mean that there is real danger.

The foundation of intervention for anxiety is the ability to challenge the message of danger and threat that feelings of anxiety are sending us. Teens need to develop the skills to coach themselves that often the situations that they are in are not nearly as threatening as their feelings make them out to be. This false alarm concept can be useful for some teens who are more flexible in thinking and benefit from the use of metaphor and learning about complex concepts. Even for teens on the spectrum with fewer abstract thinking skills, it is useful for teachers to consider this basic truth about the disconnect between irrational anxieties and objective reality. Thus, an initial key skill for teens to learn is not to buy into the panicky feelings and threatening thoughts that anxiety can sometimes cause, even in minor situations.

This anxiety intervention has two phases: skill building and then skill practice.

Phase I: Skill Building

There are four coping skills to be learned in the skill-building phase: knowing I'm nervous, irritating thoughts, calm thoughts, and keep practicing. These skills are easily remembered by the acronym KICK. The skills can be taught to students over four or five meetings.

KICK: THE FOUR COPING SKILLS TO REDUCE ANXIETY AND MELTDOWNS

K: Knowing I'm nervous

I: Irritating thoughts

C: Calm thoughts

K: Keep practicing

Knowing I'm Nervous

The first coping skill is learning how to think productively about the nature of anxiety, how it feels, and everyone's wish to reduce tension by impulsive and counterproductive actions when they are highly anxious. Teens on the spectrum are capable of learning to differentiate anxiety from other basic emotions. They can think more precisely about what anxiety is as well as what it is not. This will help them develop the ability to recognize when they have anxiety and then turn to coping skills for reducing the all-encompassing feeling of anxiety when it rises to a high level. It will enable them to think of rational, less impulsive responses to their anxious feelings. It is important that they understand that anxiety is normal (that is, everyone has it) and its relation to stress. Most important, we want to convey to them that they can cope with anxiety.

Irritating Thoughts

Once a teen learns to identify the signs of anxiety, he is ready to learn about the effects of it on his thinking patterns—the second coping skill. A core lesson for teens is that anxiety makes us believe that there is a threatening outcome that must be avoided at all costs. This anxiety is a false alarm. Because people avoid thinking about the false beliefs, they act in response to the beliefs without realizing they have them and that the beliefs are driving their behavior. For example, an adolescent who finds speaking publicly to be anxiety provoking may think of it primarily as something that he or she would rather not do. With additional structured discussion, he may be able to identify the specific threats that he imagines might be linked with his performance in the situation. For example, he might think that public speaking would lead to gossip and bullying and ultimately be a social catastrophe that will ruin his social life.

In cognitive interventions that address such irrational thoughts, the downward arrow concept of anxious beliefs (used in Lesson Plan 10.2) is helpful. The point is that anxiety makes us believe that a chain reaction of events (each worse than the last) will occur if a feared situation transpires, spiraling downward from merely unpleasant (at the top of the arrow) to deadly or damaging (at the bottom of the arrow). For example, many kids on the spectrum feel high anxiety about approaching peers to sit with at lunch even after they carefully consider approaches to peers (see Chapter Eight). Common reasons for this anxiety that many kids are able to verbalize is that they might be rejected or made to feel unwelcome. To explore this anxiety, one could (and should) ask, "What would happen next if this rejection did occur?" Following the typical stream of thoughts of the downward arrow for teens on the spectrum with social anxiety, a set of increasingly extreme assumptions is common:

- None of the kids in the group would ever want to speak with him in the future. Rumors of this humiliation would spread like wildfire to all of the other peer groups in the school, and none of them would want to associate with him either.

- The teen would therefore be friendless throughout life.

- He might fall into despair and dysfunction due to loneliness.

Certainly, teens on the spectrum often have legitimate fears of rejection based on previous experiences, which stem from their lack of social skill in selecting the most appropriate crowd to try to join. Even when they learn better social skills (for example, as a result of participation in the PEERS treatment or the guidance of teachers as in Chapter Eight), they may continue to harbor irrational anxiety about rejection and the consequences of rejection, which prevents them from approaching other kids.

It is important to compare the severity of the danger implied by the final step of this chain of thoughts (existential importance) with the basic concern that the teen initially expressed, which is that he might feel rejected. Obviously it is possible to be rejected by a single group without enduring any long-term consequences. A teen might just as easily shrug his shoulders and say, "If that's what they're like, I wouldn't have wanted them anyway." For coping effectively with anxiety, unearthing these extreme irrational beliefs about the danger of a given situation is key. There is little chance that anxiety will be reduced if these irrational beliefs remain hidden and unchallenged.

Consistent with the concept of anxiety as a false alarm, it is important to recognize that some components of our anxious beliefs are irrational and extreme. By discussing the nature of such beliefs in detail, adolescents are frequently able to recognize that their minds can distort and inflate a sense of threat to a great extent due to the false alarm from anxiety.

Calm Thoughts

In order to cope with irrational anxiety, calm thoughts are a critical skill that tweens and teens on the spectrum need to learn. Calm thoughts are direct answers to anxious thoughts and challenge the exaggerated threat that teens with high anxiety perceive. The impact of calm thoughts is twofold. First, calm thoughts challenge the probability of the perceived threat based on some kind of evidence—personal experience, observations of others, or statistics that are available through sources such as the Internet. Second, calm thoughts challenge the severity of the consequences of the perceived threat, again based on evidence and logic. Even if an unwanted event occurred, its effects and negativity would likely be limited and tolerable.

Although everyone has experienced some aspects of social embarrassment in class presentations in their lifetime, it is unlikely that these mistakes have led to long-lasting consequences in one's social life. As adolescents become skillful in the development of calm thoughts, they are able to explain this to themselves and boost their confidence.

Here's an example of a series of calm thoughts:

I've definitely made some mistakes in other performances I had to do in front of my class. I didn't like it at the time, but the truth is that almost nobody even brought it up. And when I think about it, most teens don't even care about what other teens say or do in class. They just mostly care about what kind of person you are and what you do outside class. That's what really affects your reputation. So even though I want to do a good job in all of my performances, there's a pretty low chance that making a mistake now and then is going to screw things up in my social life.

In this example, the focus is on the lack of a severe outcome even if the feared event came to pass. Evidence is central in this calm thought: the student reflects on his own experiences, as well as observations of other students, to reassure himself that the consequences are limited. By practicing calm thoughts in a variety of formats and with a variety of examples and hearing others model the use of calm thoughts as well, kids on the spectrum can pick up this skill and use it to deal with anxieties of all kinds. However, calm thoughts alone rarely immediately lead to a lessening of the physical sensations of anxiety. Like a false alarm, these sensations often continue to ring for a number of minutes or longer, even when the situation has been determined to be safe. Nevertheless, calm thoughts do often inspire a sense of confidence and a determination to not buy into the ongoing false alarm and the automatic anxious responses that go along with it.

Keep Practicing

The fourth and final coping skill for kids with anxiety to learn is to keep practicing by taking small steps. Students on the spectrum with anxiety issues must learn to slowly face fears and engage in behaviors that trigger anxiety. In this way, they can teach their brains that many situations they worry about are actually safe. Taking small steps rather than attempting to make big changes all at once can reverse panic reactions. This ensures a smooth transition from an anxious to a more confident way of thinking and acting.

Once adolescents master the general idea of taking small steps and practicing in one or two sample situations, they can generalize this skill to a variety of other anxiety-producing situations. Exposing themselves to tolerable levels of fear and anxiety can become a coping skill that teens on the spectrum can initiate themselves in future anxious situations. They therefore learn to face a little fear to fight a big fear.

Phase II: Practicing the Skills

This concept of small steps is the transitional point leading to the second phase of the intervention. In this phase, students face some fears, initially in small doses, in order to get hands-on experience with the four coping skills they have learned. Beginning with mildly anxiety-provoking situations, students on the spectrum can build up to facing more significant fears once they have achieved some initial confidence. For example, if the issue is public speaking anxiety, a series of class presentations beginning with a three-sentence speech given to the teacher and one student, and read from a script, might be the first step to significantly longer, less-prompted presentations in front of the entire class. Multiple steps are often necessary, but these exercises in facing fears can be a powerful catalyst of change in a teen's anxious beliefs about almost any situation. Research shows that facing fears in small steps leads to the greatest anxiety reduction—even more than emotion and thought recognition training. Thus, it is important to leave time for this aspect of the anxiety curriculum in whatever format it is ultimately presented to the student or class.

It is also helpful for teachers to recognize that a parent-administered incentive program can be highly beneficial in promoting the teen's adherence and engagement in this phase. (This is discussed in the lesson plans that follow.) However, even without an explicit incentive program, teachers can keep teens engaged in this curriculum by assigning homework and treating the lesson plans as they would any other lesson in their classroom, expecting students' full attention.

In sum, teachers can introduce these four basic KICK coping skills in separate lessons to teens over the course of the intervention. These skills can lead to significant improvement in anxiety problems for most teens on the spectrum.

Lesson Plans

We present lesson plans for Phases I and II and an incentive program involving the student and parents. Each lesson plan has relevant handouts for students and parents. Parent handouts may be sent home for informational purposes to promote wraparound support for anxiety issues in the home environment as well. The incentive program addresses both facing fears and managing meltdowns and outbursts. Behavioral management is always a challenge in such cases. However, careful use of these research-proven incentive programs can have significant beneficial effects on the reduction of outbursts in the context of the other anxiety management skills that are taught to the students.

Each of these lessons can be accomplished in a thirty- to sixty-minute meeting, although individual teaching styles and group needs may dictate shorter or longer durations for each lesson for full comprehension and mastery to occur.

LESSON PLAN 10.1 Emotion Recognition: "Knowing I'm Nervous"

SELECTED STUDENT NEED

- Identifying signs of anxiety and differentiating it from other emotions.

LEARNING OBJECTIVES

- Students will be able to differentiate facial expressions and body postures associated with anxiety from those associated with other emotions.
- Students will recognize that there are several common physical symptoms that most people experience when they are anxious.

STANDARDS AND BENCHMARKS

- Distinguish facial expressions associated with anxiety from those associated with other emotions.
- Notice physical sensations of anxiety in daily life situations.

MATERIALS AND RESOURCES

- Review the anxiety assessments that have been administered to the youth on the spectrum and their parents, as well as the anxiety questionnaire you completed regarding this student (Handout 9.1). This is intended to refresh your memory for this student's particular anxiety issues.

Introduction

In the first class, the main goal is to develop students' ability to understand and interpret emotional cues. Teens on the spectrum have difficulty identifying their own emotional state and need to become familiar with the concept that the body (through sensations and facial expressions) sends the teen and those around him important messages about the emotions he or she is experiencing.

The Class Session

Start with, "Today we are going to learn about different emotions, especially anxiety. I have had all of you fill out a form listing different types of emotions and behaviors. Now we are going to learn more about how to tell the difference between the emotions, and especially what happens in our brains and bodies when we experience anxiety."

LESSON PLAN 10.1   (continued)

Identifying Emotions

Draw a large smiley face on the board. Then draw a face with a frown, wide eyes, and raised eyebrows. Then draw a frowning face with a teardrop. Finally, draw a frowning face with squinting eyes and eyebrows angled diagonally. Ask the class if there are any artists who would like to embellish the pictures and offer volunteers chalk or markers and erasers. Before they make alterations, ask the class to identify each emotion, state what is unique about the accompanying facial expression, and suggest additional details. Have each volunteer artist first label the emotions accurately in writing. Then have them make additions to your basic drawings that are consistent with the facial expressions for each emotion. For example, for happiness, it is fine to add wrinkles around the eye, dimpled cheeks, and an open laughing mouth. As a guide, these are the most common elements for facial expressions and body posture:

EMOTION	CUES
Fear ("scared," "nervous," "afraid," "anxious")	Wide eyes; sometimes a frown; sometimes an open mouth; raised eyebrows; shivering; sweating
Anger	Squinting; angled eyebrows; furrowed brow ("wrinkly forehead"); pursed lips; red face
Sadness	Crying; frown; drooping shoulders; slumped over (head in hands); looking away from others
Happiness	Smile/grin; laughing; wrinkles on the sides of eyes

- Introduce the idea that bodily posture and other cues can also be hall-marks of the various emotions. Ask for additional volunteers to draw the postures of a happy person and a scared person. Provide clarifi-cation, as necessary, to help the students identify the visual cues that inform us about others' emotions. For example, you might say, "What about the body in particular tells us that she is feeling scared? Is there something about her mouth that gives us clues? What about her eyes and eyebrows? Okay, so let's review. What are the main ways we can tell that someone is scared from looking at his or her face and body? And how does that differ, from, say, happiness?"

- Focus on the four basic emotions: fear, anger, sadness, and happiness. Some students may also want to distinguish between surprise (which usually has a gape-mouthed feature) and fear. Others may want to add more complex emotions, such as jealousy. Allow them to do so briefly to encourage participation, but ensure they understand the key features of the four basic emotions.

- Help the students understand that when it comes to fear, there are different words for the same feeling: *feeling afraid, scared, nervous, worried,* or *anxious.* They all mean the same thing. Ask which words the students use. Be sure to use these words in the future in discussing fear and anxiety.

- Play a game of charades. Model one of the four basic emotions, and ask students to guess your feeling. Then ask for volunteers to model emotions. Encourage students to make some easier and some harder to guess. Point out that emotions can come across subtly, but that they are nevertheless distinguishable and relatively unique in presentation.

Identifying Anxiety: The K Step

- Share a situation with your students that causes even adults modest anxiety that is socially acceptable, such as going on a roller coaster (avoid examples such as driving on highways, which might model novel anxious thoughts for the students that could have an impact on their daily functioning). Use yourself as an example. It's best to provide a slightly theatrical or humorous description of your experience to engage and maintain the students' interest and attention. Describe the physical cues that the situation elicited for you: racing heart, trembling, sweating, fast breathing, stomachache, light-headedness, and headache, for example. You might say, "The only time I went on an upside-down roller coaster, my friend had to practically drag me into the cart because I couldn't get the idea of danger out of my mind. As soon as we started going up the first hill, my heart started beating so fast I thought everyone in the whole amusement park could hear it along with my hyperventilation."

- Briefly point out that the reason we feel this way is that the brain releases adrenaline into the bloodstream when we become anxious. Adrenaline causes all of these other feelings—stomachache, tension, light-headedness, and so forth.

- Students may volunteer describing their experiences in a feared situation when they were younger to promote their willingness to share personal events. Help each student think about the kinds of physical symptoms and bodily reactions he had (tension, trembling, sweating, stomachache, and so forth). Ask rhetorically if these body sensations are one way we can tell when we are afraid. Follow up by noting, "Yes, the way our body feels is a very easy way we can tell if we're afraid, nervous, or anxious."

- Reinforce the concept of using physical cues as a signal of approaching anxiety: "Before we know what to do about anxiety, we have to know when we're becoming anxious. We refer to this as the K step: knowing I'm nervous."

- Write KICK vertically on the board and fill in the K step: "Knowing I'm nervous." Explain to the class that they're going to be learning the KICK plan as a way to feel better when they become afraid. That's what this lesson is about.

- Say, as you draw an "inverted U" mountain and a stick figure person on the board:

  Let's practice. Let's say a person didn't like going up to high places. And then he had to go to the top of a mountain and look down. Then he started shivering and sweating. His eyes got really wide-open. [Quickly draw squiggles and circles to represent shivers, sweat, and wide eyes.] How do you think he is feeling? How can you tell? Why don't you think he's happy? Why not sad?

- Ask if the students can think of something that would make most teens afraid, and list these suggestions on the board. Common examples that teens generate are "asking someone on a date," "going to a school dance stag," and "saying something embarrassing in front of a group of kids you don't know well." Aim to generate a list of three to ten appropriate teen-suggested anxieties, with examples given as needed.

- Some teens may want to focus on dares, such as climbing to the school roof. Respond by acknowledging that these situations would certainly make teens scared if they had to do the dare, but that dares are usually bad ideas that we can choose not to do. Reframe this point by noting that what really makes teens nervous is having the courage to stand up to a risky dare and refusing to take it. It can be helpful to explore why people are afraid of humiliation in front of their peers and can lack the self-confidence to stand up for themselves when they face a dare. Throughout this lesson, ignore answers about emotions that are wrong or insincere. This topic can be difficult for some teens and make others uncomfortable. Focus your attention on those who are providing accurate and interesting remarks about identifying anxiety.

LESSON PLAN 10.1   (continued)

Homework Assignment

Explain the assignment in this way:

> In order to help you with the skill of noticing the signs of anxiety, your homework assignment is to make up a story about a teen who was in one of these situations [point to the board with the list of anxious situations that the students suggested]. You can draw a set of stick-figure cartoons for the story or write a one- to two-page short story. Your story must explain what made the teenager anxious and illustrate what physical sensations he or she was experiencing during the anxiety. Also, be sure to explain or show how people could tell the teen was afraid by looking at him.

Assessment

Note the students' accuracy in identifying both the physical sensations and facial expressions of the characters in their short stories or drawings. Repeat this lesson until accuracy is at 90 percent for students on the spectrum.

Social Skills Success for Students with Autism/Asperger's, copyright © 2011 John Wiley and Sons, Inc.

LESSON PLAN 10.2 False Alarms and Irritating Thoughts

SELECTED STUDENT NEED

- Learning how anxiety is triggered by irrational thoughts about danger.

LEARNING OBJECTIVES

- Students will understand the concept of anxiety as a false alarm.
- Students will be able to identify at least one situation that can cause teens to feel anxious even though they are not in any danger.
- Students will be able to give examples of irritating thoughts that cause anxiety.

STANDARDS AND BENCHMARKS

- Distinguish normal anxiety when there are real problems from anxiety caused by false alarms.
- Notice anxious thoughts in daily life situations.

MATERIALS AND RESOURCES

- The teen homework assignment from the previous lesson. Write this assignment on the board in advance to be completed as part of students' daily class homework.
- Handout 10.1, "Parent Information Letter About Anxiety Curriculum: False Alarms and Irritating Thoughts" information letter. Send this to parents to keep them updated on this week's anxiety topic.

Introduction

In this second lesson about anxiety, the main goal is to teach students about false alarms and how they can be caused by unrealistic beliefs about danger. Teens on the spectrum have difficulty thinking about mental processes, such as their own thoughts. They need to become familiar with the idea that feelings of anxiety, such as tension and nausea, come from beliefs about serious consequences (for example, dying or lifelong problems) that are often unrealistic.

Be sure to encourage any spontaneous self-disclosure about anxieties that students make. Normalize the anxiety by pointing out that most teens have felt that way at some point. Discourage any critical remarks peers may make, and reinforce the students who disclose for having the courage to admit something that everyone has in some form or another: anxiety. Hearing these disclosures is very helpful to students on the spectrum, so your goal is to create a class environment that is open to them. By using the mixed modalities of drawing, writing, and talking, as well as giving interesting age-appropriate examples,

LESSON PLAN 10.2 (continued)

students on the spectrum are likely to be engaged. This multisensory teaching approach will also improve their comprehension of the material.

If you only have thirty minutes for this lesson, break this plan into two separate thirty-minute sessions: one on false alarms and the other on irritating thoughts. There is a lot to cover, and sixty minutes will allow enough time to discuss it sufficiently.

The Class Session

Start with, "Today we are going to learn about how feelings of anxiety—like getting tense and uptight—get triggered because we believe that things are going to turn out badly. When we get scared and anxious, it is often like a false alarm. We feel that things are really dangerous, but actually, there's nothing much to worry about. So we are going to learn more about false alarms and how they come from our thoughts and beliefs."

False Alarms

- In stick-figure detail, draw a bedside table with a large old-fashioned alarm clock (with visible bells and a clock face) across the room from a bed with a person lying on it. Draw the big and little hands of the clock pointing at 6:30, and in a different color (preferably red), draw a single alarm hand pointing at 6:30 as well. Explain this clock to the students briefly and ask what happens at 6:30 A.M. (The alarm goes off.) Draw several curved lines over the alarm bells indicating it is going off. Explain that this is good, because the student needs to get up for school at 6:30 A.M. Ask rhetorically, "So what does the bell going off make the student do, and why? ... Yes, that's right. The ringing sound is really annoying, so it makes him want to get out of bed and shut it off. Once he's out of bed, the day begins."

- Now change the alarm hand to point to 2:30. Explain that the student set the alarm clock incorrectly the night before. Ask the students what would happen. "Exactly. The alarm forces the student to get out of bed again. But then he realizes that it is 2:30 A.M., not 6:30 A.M. It is a false alarm, but it forced him to do the same thing that he does when he really does need to get up. Guess what? Now he's having a hard time getting back to sleep." Ask the students why this is a problem. Make the point that the false alarm made him take an unnecessary action that ended up ruining his sleep. We all know how hard it is to have a good day at school when we're exhausted. In this case, the false alarm was a real nuisance. Keep this picture on the board for now.

- Introduce the idea that anxiety, fear, nervousness, or any other word the students prefer to describe this emotion can be like a true alarm or a false alarm too. Make two lists on the board labeled "True Alarm" and "False Alarm." Give examples of each, such as being chased by a bear, seeing a car driving toward you as you cross the street, and seeing thick smoke coming from one of the classrooms (true alarms), versus calling a new friend for the first time, acting in a class play, or feeling nervous learning to drive a car in an empty parking lot (false alarms). Point out that many people feel anxious when they are about to do the activities on the false alarm list and give an example: "Imagine a teen sitting with his cell phone in his hand, not quite dialing the number, wondering if the new friend will actually want to talk to him." Note that the three examples given here as false alarms are in the domain of social and generalized anxieties. If the teen on the spectrum has significant separation anxiety issues, an example might be given of a teen who was nervous about going away on a class trip overnight or a summer program in a different state away from home—examples that illustrate separation anxiety that wouldn't seem too immature to other teens.

- Ask the students for a few reasons that teens might get scared about the other situations on the false alarm list. Detailed responses are not needed for now, just basic explanations of the cause of the anxiety (for example, a worry that the boy or girl asked would turn down the date). The students can also suggest a few more examples for the false alarm list.

- Make the point that although teens often worry about these kinds of situations, things often work out fine. Ask: "How many teens actually crash their parents' car in an empty parking lot the first time they practice driving? . . . . Right! It basically doesn't happen!" Illustrate that this is what is meant by *false alarm*. People can feel very scared in situations that are completely safe.

- Draw a parallel with the alarm clock scenario: "Remember how this teen was forced by his alarm clock to wake up at 2:30 A.M. to turn it off, even though it was a false alarm? Feelings of anxiety and nervousness also often make us take actions, even when they are a false alarm. For instance, the teen feeling anxious about calling the new friend couldn't quite get himself to dial the number. The anxiety told him to avoid the danger of calling, even though there was really no danger."

- Ask the students why this example of delaying making the phone call is a problem. The main point is that it is a waste of time to worry about whether to call. The teen ends up feeling tension and other sensations that are unpleasant, and the friend most likely would like to talk if he's free.

- Encourage the students to suggest ways that the other situations on the false alarm list caused the teens to act. For example, the teen who worried about crashing the car might avoid practicing driving or might drive extremely slowly.

- Point out that although there is no reason to feel so nervous in false alarm situations, the anxiety and nervousness that the teens feel are just as intense and uncomfortable as their feelings in true alarm situations (for example, being chased by the bear). Just like the alarm clock that rings accidentally at 2:30 A.M. and makes us get out of bed, the anxiety and nervousness make us behave timidly and feel uncomfortable, even when there is nothing really to worry about.

Irritating Thoughts: The I Step

- Refer to the situation that you mentioned in the first lesson that causes even adults modest anxiety, such as going on roller coasters. Again, use yourself as an example with a slightly humorous attitude about the experience. Remind students of your physical cues in the situation indicating anxiety (your racing heart, for example). Point out that this is a good example of a false alarm situation. Draw a stick figure of yourself in the situation. Ask the class if they can guess what you were afraid of. Pay attention to appropriate responses that accurately convey a possible belief about danger (for example, fear of falling out of the roller-coaster cart). Draw a thought bubble touching the head of the cartoon figure of yourself and paraphrase the students' suggestions in first-person language in writing inside the thought bubble—for example, "I am afraid I'm gonna fall out and croak!"

- Ask for a volunteer to draw one or more of the false alarm situations discussed earlier in class—perhaps the student who feels afraid of driving for the first time.

- With the drawings as props, discuss with the class what kinds of thoughts the students may have had in these false alarm situations—for example: "I could crash this car since it's my first time driving," "My new friend will blow me off and not want to talk," or "I could turn out to be a horrible actor and totally embarrass myself in the school play." Have the student write the suggested thoughts in thought bubbles in first-person language.

- Introduce the downward arrow concept. Draw an arrow from the top to bottom of the board, pointing down. Note that when we are anxious, we believe that something could go wrong, but we often don't pay attention to the specifics of our beliefs. In our subconscious mind, where we think but aren't aware of our thoughts, are a lot of fearful thoughts that sometimes make us much more scared than we should be. Use a social anxiety example, like the teen who is afraid of calling a new friend. Near the top of the arrow, write the initial anxious thought, such as, "My new friend wouldn't want to talk to me when I call." Emphasize that this is probably just the tip of the iceberg. The next question to ask is, "If that happened, what would happen next?" With class participation, generate a set of three to five additional thoughts for additional steps of the chain of thoughts, each worse than the last. Emphasize that it does not have to be rational or reflect what every teen might think in the situation—just some teens. We all have our own set of anxieties. Write each additional thought below the last, next to the arrow—for example:

My new friend wouldn't want to talk to me when I call.	
It means that he's actually not a friend.	
That means I probably won't be able to make any new friends.	
That would mean that I will start losing my old friends when they see no one else likes me.	
I'll end up being a total outcast for the rest of high school.	

- Point out that each thought along the downward arrow gets more extreme than the previous one and that most people are not even aware that they have such extreme thoughts. Yet these thoughts cause the unpleasant feelings of anxiety and unnecessary caution.

- Repeat the downward arrow technique with one or two additional false alarm situations that were already discussed today.

- Now present the I step: irritating thoughts. Write the letters KICK in large block letters on the board. Fill in the first two steps of the acronym: K—Knowing I'm Nervous and I—Irritating Thoughts. Ask how students can know they are nervous from Lesson 10.1 (feelings of tension, nausea, facial expressions, body posture, desire not to do something). Point out that once we know we are nervous in the K step, the second step, I, is to figure out our irritating thoughts about the situation. Point to the examples with the downward arrow presented on the board. All of the thoughts written beside the arrow are irritating and make us feel that something bad could happen. The bottom, most extreme thought is particularly irritating because it

LESSON PLAN 10.2 (continued)

really makes us anxious and sounds as if things could be a disaster. Until we figure out our most extreme anxious thoughts, we won't be able to make ourselves feel any better (that is the topic of Lesson Plan 10.3), because we will still believe we are in danger.

- As in Lesson Plan 10.1, ignore insincere answers. By listening to and encouraging students who are participating sincerely, you will set a good emotional tone to help the class tolerate their own anxiety in these lessons.

Homework Assignment

Explain the assignment:

In order to help you practice identifying irritating thoughts, your homework assignment is to write or draw about a time, any time, in your life when you were scared. It can be either a true alarm situation—when you had a good reason to be scared—or a false alarm, where it turned out to be no big deal. Either way, write about or show the situation, what happened to you, and then describe or show how you could tell you felt anxious (how your body showed the anxiety), and, even more important, what your irritating thoughts were. Try to draw a downward arrow like we did in class and show a chain of irritating thoughts that go from bad to worse—at least four of them. If you draw a picture, use a thought bubble for this.

Note the students' accuracy in distinguishing false alarm situations from true alarm situations, as well as their ability to identify unrealistic anxious beliefs (irritating thoughts). Repeat this lesson until accuracy is at 90 percent for students on the spectrum.

HANDOUT 10.1 Parent Information Letter About Anxiety Curriculum: False Alarms and Irritating Thoughts

Dear Parents:

In our anxiety education lesson today, we focused on the concepts of false alarms and irritating (anxious) thoughts. Everyone experiences some anxiety, but sometimes anxiety can be quite unrealistic and unnecessary.

Many parents are curious about where such anxiety comes from. One primary factor is the temperament that people are born with. Temperament is just an individual's emotional style—how easy it is for that person to experience certain emotions. Adolescents vary a lot in terms of their typical reaction to events in their lives. Some adolescents have feelings of anxiety triggered easily, especially when they are in unfamiliar situations or are stressed out. It can take relatively little to cause their brain to set off a rush of adrenaline that ends up making them feel tense and anxious. This leads to many false alarms, when adolescents get nervous and wound up over issues that are manageable or even inconsequential. Examples we discussed in class include calling a new friend, learning to drive, and acting in a school play.

Anxiety makes us believe that a set of events, each worse than the previous one, could occur. For example, students in a new school often feel high anxiety about approaching classmates at lunchtime. A common reason for this anxiety is that they believe they might be rejected. To explore this anxiety, one could ask, "What would happen next if this did occur?" A typical set of thoughts for many adolescents might be: this would mean (1) that none of their friends in the group would want to speak with him or her in the future; (2) that rumors of this humiliation would spread to the other peer groups in the school, and none of them would want to hang out with the teen either; and (3) that the student would be friendless for life. Often adolescents aren't even aware of the extreme nature of their own thoughts until they learn to explore just how bad they believe things might get (when they are feeling anxious).

Recognizing these kinds of beliefs about danger is key for coping effectively with anxiety. There is little chance that anxiety can be reduced if adolescents don't challenge these beliefs. We'll be working on learning to do that next week.

Sincerely,

LESSON PLAN 10.3 Calm Thoughts

SELECTED STUDENT NEED

- Learning how to manage anxiety by challenging irrational thoughts about danger.

LEARNING OBJECTIVE

- Students will be able to identify realistic (calm) thoughts to challenge anxious beliefs.

STANDARDS AND BENCHMARKS

- Accurately verbalize calm thoughts that effectively challenge anxious beliefs based on evidence or logic.
- Employ calm thoughts when needed in daily life situations.

MATERIALS AND RESOURCES

- Teen homework assignment from the previous lesson. Write the assignment on the board in advance, to be completed as part of students' daily class homework.
- Handout 10.2, "Parent Information Letter About Anxiety Curriculum: Calm Thoughts." Send this to parents to keep them updated on this week's anxiety topic.

Introduction

In this third anxiety lesson, the main goal is to teach students how to challenge their unrealistic beliefs about danger. Teens on the spectrum can develop expertise in this skill by thinking of it as a chance to prove something with evidence. Although unrealistic beliefs cause anxiety, teens do not have to buy into these beliefs. They can disprove the beliefs and give themselves a boost of confidence to face their fears. As with the previous lesson, be sure to encourage any spontaneous self-disclosure about fears and anxieties that any students make. These may be incorporated into the lesson itself, say, as examples for generating irritating and calm thoughts if the students are self-confident and willing.

The Class Session

Start with, "Today we are going to learn about fighting back against irritating thoughts. Irritating thoughts make us feel anxious, like something terrible could happen, even when things are totally safe. They cause a false alarm—they get us tense and worried for no good reason and make us want to avoid situations that are probably fun. We can either listen to the false alarm and do what it wants us to do, or we can reset the alarm so it goes off only when we're truly in danger. Today we're going learn a skill for doing that. The skill is to challenge irritating thoughts with evidence."

LESSON PLAN 10.3   (continued)

Review K and I Steps

- As with the first two lessons, write the letters KICK in large block letters on the board. Fill in the phrases for the K and I steps: K—Knowing I'm Nervous and I—Irritating Thoughts. Review how students can tell that they are feeling anxiety (they feel tension, are light-headed, or something else). Remind them that this anxiety sends them a powerful message: be cautious, get out of here, don't do the feared activity, and avoid. Continue: "However, when we get these anxious feelings, we need to figure out why. That is the I step. Our irritating thoughts are telling us what we believe about the situation, even if these beliefs are totally wrong. Let's review a few examples."

- Suggest a common irrational teen anxiety, such as fearing rejection when asking someone to a school dance. Ask for a volunteer to draw a brief sketch of the situation on the board and be sure to show anxiety in the facial expression and posture. Then ask the student to add a large thought bubble on one side of the picture.

- Using the downward arrow technique described in Lesson Plan 10.2, engage the students in generating three to five increasingly anxious thoughts about the situation. Write these thoughts in the thought bubble.

- Repeat this process with an additional cartoon on a separate topic. Try to orient this topic to the primary anxiety area (social, generalized, or separation) experienced by the teen on the autism spectrum. Examples from the false alarm lesson could be used. Other examples are a teen scared to give a speech for a class election, a teen nervous about taking a trip out of town with his class, or a teen worried about an upcoming essay test. Leave substantial room between the two pictures on the board. These two pictures will serve as the basis for learning calm thoughts.

Calm Thoughts

- Add the phrase "Calm Thoughts" to the "C" step of the KICK acronym you wrote on the board earlier. Explain the concept: that calm thoughts challenge and disprove irritating thoughts. This is easiest to explain by starting with the irritating thoughts at the bottom of the downward arrow and asking, "How likely would this be to happen?" Then continue:

  Let's go back to the teen who was worried that this girl would turn him down if he asked her to the dance. Remember, you just

LESSON PLAN 10.3 (continued)

said that his most irritating thought would be that all the other kids would find out and laugh at him, and he'd end up an outcast and a social reject for the rest of high school. Now, since you guys are pretty experienced with the way social life works in high school by now, I would ask you: How likely is this to actually happen? Have you ever heard of someone's entire high school social life being ruined because someone turned him down for a date? One date? I mean, no friends, outcast? Come on.

- Use a humorous tone when presenting the initial counterarguments to irritating thoughts. Teens benefit from being able to laugh off their anxieties, and modeling this attitude from the start helps.

- Allow the students to discuss this topic for a minute and focus your attention on responses that take a rational approach to the matter—for example, that although it's easy to worry about these terrible outcomes, it would be extremely unlikely. Build off that point if the opportunity permits, or introduce it yourself. The idea is to get the students thinking in statistical terms: "Okay, so, you go to a high school with about two thousand students. How many students in this high school do you figure have ever had someone turn them down for a dance at least once?" Solicit multiple responses from the students; often there will be lots of opinions: "That's right. No one knows for sure, but the truth is that this happens all the time. And of course, it has probably never ruined anyone's social life. So what are the chances of this [irritating thought] actually happening? One out of a hundred? A thousand?"

- Two types of calm thoughts are helpful: (1) How likely is the irritating thought to actually happen? and (2) If it did happen, how bad would it be? Often one of these types of calm thoughts is more appropriate than the other for a given situation. The first question can make teens feel better when they know that something almost never happens (for example, a teen failing out of high school because of doing poorly on one essay test—"It's never happened to anyone else, right? How likely is it to happen to me?"). The second question is more appropriate when teens think something "a little bad" could actually happen, but that it would not be the end of the world—for example, making a mistake during a speech: "If I mess up, nobody will really care, so does it really matter? Most teens don't care much about what you do or say in a speech anyway. In the case of the school dance scenario, the likelihood of a ruined social life is very low. Also, while being turned down would disappoint anyone, we'd probably get over it quickly because we all have things in life that can cheer us up quickly: our pets, our family, friends, and lots more."

170

LESSON PLAN 10.3   (continued)

- Refresh the student's memory about the teen who was feeling shy about calling a new friend from the lesson on false alarms. On the board, draw a two-column chart like the irritating thoughts chart, and fill in the irritating thoughts that were generated in the previous lesson on the left-hand side. Then, soliciting class participation as much as possible, generate calm thoughts to enter into the right-hand column. These thoughts should be based on the two types of questions noted: how likely something is to happen, and how bad it would actually be if it did happen. Point out that students should use evidence from their own lives, observations, or material they have read or things they have heard to make calm thoughts. Sometimes the evidence is a fact or sometimes an educated guess. Either way, having evidence to challenge each irritating thought is much better at reducing anxiety than just saying something generic like, "Everything will be okay." Here's what the final scenario might look like:

My new friend doesn't want to talk when I call.	Even if she doesn't want to, so what? She is probably busy right now. Maybe her mom just yelled at her. Maybe she's not into the phone. I could tell her to call or text me when she's free.	
It means that she's actually not a friend.	That's not very likely, because we're already planning to go to the mall this weekend. So I know we're already kinda friends. Even if we don't end up being close friends, so what? There're two thousand other kids at this school.	
That means I probably won't be able to make any new friends.	That's not very likely because I've made new friends in the past. There are plenty of kids I could make friends with here.	
That would mean that I will start losing my old friends when they see no one else likes me.	That is so unlikely. The reason my old friends are my friends is that I can count on them. They don't care who else I hang out with. I've had them for years. Why would I lose them over something little like this?	
I'll end up being a total outcast for the rest of high school.	I've never heard of that happening to anyone, so it is about a one out of a million chance to happen to me.	

LESSON PLAN 10.3   (continued)

- Reinforce the concept of the C step: Calm thoughts. "After we know we're nervous and have figured out our actual, most serious, irritating thoughts, we should develop calm thoughts that challenge the irritating thoughts. That gives us a boost of confidence, because we know there is evidence to prove that there is nothing worth worrying about. Our feelings of anxiety may slowly begin to fade. But the feelings can stay around a little longer because the adrenaline stays in our system for awhile before it runs out. Even while we still feel a bit nervous, we know we don't have to buy into the false alarm when we have accurate calm thoughts."

Homework Assignment

Explain the assignment:

In order to help you practice calm thoughts, your homework assignment is to take your story or picture from last week—about a time when you were anxious—and make calm thoughts to challenge each of the irritating thoughts that you thought of. Remember that calm thoughts prove that the irritating thoughts are unlikely to happen, or that if they did happen, it wouldn't be a big deal. Be sure to use evidence, like your own experience or things you've heard or read, in your calm thoughts. You can either add calm thoughts to what you wrote last week, or put it in a thought bubble in your picture if you drew one.

Assessment

Note the students' ability to identify calm thoughts that use specific evidence to refute anxious beliefs. Repeat this lesson until accuracy is at 90 percent for students on the spectrum.

Social Skills Success for Students with Autism/Asperger's, copyright © 2011 John Wiley and Sons, Inc.

HANDOUT 10.2 Parent Information Letter About Anxiety Curriculum: Calm Thoughts

Dear Parents:

In our anxiety education lesson today, we focused on the concept of calm thoughts. As we learned last week, anxiety makes people believe that a set of events, each worse than the last, could occur. Often these beliefs are not very rational, but people believe them because they have never tried to challenge or disprove the beliefs.

Calm thoughts are direct answers to anxious, irritating thoughts. They challenge the likelihood that our fearful beliefs will come true based on some kind of evidence: personal experience, observations of others, or information available through sources like the Internet. Calm thoughts can also challenge the consequences of a fearful belief: even if an unwanted event occurred, its negative effects are often tolerable.

For example, although everyone has experienced some aspects of social embarrassment in public speaking in their lifetime, it is almost universally the case that none of these mistakes have led to long-lasting consequences. As adolescents become skillful in the development of calm thoughts, they are able to generate in their own words how to make these kinds of points for themselves. Once they become skilled at calm thoughts, they can talk themselves out of a lot of unnecessary anxiety.

Here is an example of a series of calm thoughts challenging a student's worries about giving a speech in class: "I've definitely made some mistakes in other speeches I had to do in class. I didn't like it at the time, but the truth is that almost nobody even brought it up to me. Most kids don't care that much about what other kids say in class. They mostly care about what kind of person you are and what you do outside class. So even though I want to do a good job in my speech, there's a pretty low chance that making a mistake is going to screw things up in my social life."

In this example, the point is that even if the feared event happened, the consequences wouldn't be bad. The student uses evidence in this calm thought; he reflects on his own experiences, as well as observations of other students, to reassure himself. By practicing calm thoughts with a variety of examples, kids can pick up this skill and use it to deal with anxieties of all kinds. It can help adolescents to hear their parents give examples of calm thoughts from situations in their lives, too.

Sincerely,

LESSON PLAN 10.4 Small Steps

SELECTED STUDENT NEED
- Learning how to manage anxiety by taking small steps in facing fears.

LEARNING OBJECTIVE
- Students will be able to identify a hierarchy of small steps to address a specific fear.

STANDARDS AND BENCHMARKS
- Accurately verbalize the rationale for taking small steps in facing fears.
- Break down fearful situations into small steps when needed in daily life.

MATERIALS AND RESOURCES
- Teen homework assignment from the previous lesson. Write the assignment on the board in advance, to be completed as part of students' daily class homework.
- Handout 10.3, "Parent Information Letter About Anxiety Curriculum: Keep Practicing by Taking Small Steps." Send this to parents to keep them updated on this week's anxiety topic.

Introduction

In the fourth anxiety lesson, the primary goal is to teach students about the concept of breaking fearful situations into small steps. Teens can prove to themselves that they can handle feared situations by trying things out a bit at a time and slowly gaining confidence as they build up to more challenging steps. This process gives teens experience with success that helps them challenge their irritating thoughts more effectively. Taking small steps also keeps teens from panicking at any given step. This is the key to overcoming specific fears and getting over ingrained patterns of avoidance. Once again, it is beneficial if students voluntarily share their own anxieties, so be sure to leave time to discuss such comments at a comfortable level of detail to process the anxieties sufficiently. The example of learning to swim is useful to begin with because it is such a universal experience that illustrates this point especially clearly.

The Class Session

Start with, "Today we are going to learn about fighting back against anxiety by facing our fears in small steps. Last week we learned to give ourselves a boost of confidence by using calm thoughts, so we know there is nothing serious to fear. This week we are going to take the next step and prove to ourselves that there is nothing to fear by trying things out gradually."

Social Skills Success for Students with Autism/Asperger's, copyright © 2011 John Wiley and Sons, Inc.

LESSON PLAN 10.4 (continued)

Small Steps

- Point out that the most important step to take after developing calm thoughts is to figure out how to break a feared situation into small steps. Here's an example: "If a child hasn't been in a swimming pool before, she would probably be scared to jump in the deep end by herself where she couldn't keep her head above water on her own. What small steps would she take to build up to swimming in the deep end, beginning with just putting her feet in the water?" Encourage the class to come up with at least four or five steps of learning to swim for a child. These can be written on the board in order to exemplify the idea of a series of steps.

- Introduce the idea of a feelings thermometer. Draw a simple thermometer on the board with a range of 0 to 10 like the following:

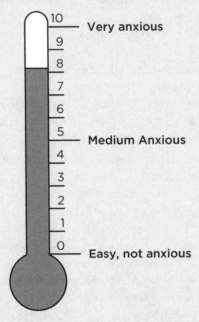

- Ask the class to guess how the child would rate going in the deep end by herself if she had never been in the pool before. "Right! If she was at all sensible, she would rate it as a 9 or a 10! In this case, she is smart to be anxious. She's not ready for that; she needs to take smaller steps to get there." Ask what step might be around a 0 or 1 on the anxiety scale for a typical child who was just learning to swim (maybe putting her toes in the water). Taking the students' examples of intermediate steps, have them rate how the girl would feel about each of them before she had ever been in the pool. Perhaps standing in the water

might be around a 2 to 4, having a parent hold her in a swimming position might be a bit higher, and putting her head under water for the
first time would be over a 5.

- Ask the class, "Once the girl has learned to swim well, how would these
ratings change?" The point is that steps that were once considered
very anxiety provoking, like putting her head under water or even
jumping off a diving board, might now be rated as 0 or at least very
low. Getting experience with something anxiety provoking by taking
small steps can teach our brains not to worry anymore; it can make the
anxiety go away or at least go way down.

- Now take a teen-relevant situation that has been of interest to the class
in previous lessons—for example, asking someone to the dance, calling
a new friend, fear of taking an essay test or an overnight class trip—and
practice breaking it down into small steps in the same way, using the
feelings thermometer as a guide for which steps come first. Tell the
class to assume that a teen is feeling very anxious about the feared
situation—perhaps 9 out of 10 on the anxiety scale. Write that situation next to the 9 on the feelings thermometer: "Asking the girl to go to
the dance." "We need to figure out small steps for this guy to take so
he can build up to this. If it is a 9, he may not be ready to start up there.
Let's think of some things he can do to build up his confidence."

- The development of appropriate small steps to face fears is an
acquired skill. It helps to think of trivial acts that would be rated as 0
or 1 to begin with and see where the logical progression of slightly
harder steps goes from there. For example, for the dance situation,
a sample series of steps might be: 0, make eye contact with the girl
and smile slightly in class; 2, ask her what time it is; 4, call her to ask
about a homework assignment; 6, approach her when she's walking
alone at school and ask her a question about something interesting
she has with her; 8, get advice from friends about whether to ask her
based on all the steps taken so far; 9, if it's looking good, ask her to the
dance. Even though the last step is rated originally as a 9 (very anxiety
provoking), that rating could go down somewhat if all of the other
initial steps went well.

LESSON PLAN 10.4 (continued)

- Repeat this for a situation relevant to the anxieties experienced by the teen on the spectrum (either a social, generalized, or separation anxiety example using the assessment from Chapter Nine).

- Many activities that initially seem difficult or fearful to some teens to begin with (like a month-long sleep-away camp) can seem very easy to them after they do it. Ask the students if they have any examples from their own lives of activities that they have mastered that might have seemed difficult or fearful to begin with. Encourage them to think of any intermediate steps they took to build up to the task. Add remarks like the following, as appropriate: "For example, it is a good idea to practice a few overnight sleepovers with a friend before trying to go to an overnight summer camp for a month, right?"

- If students give some examples of tasks that scared them that they just "did anyway," without taking any intermediate small steps, ask the class how other teens in the same situation could practice, that is, use small steps to get used to the situation before building up to the real thing. Point out that if our anxiety is not too high, it is fine to skip over some of the small steps, but if our anxiety is over a 4 or 5, small steps really help build confidence.

Present the Last K Step: Keep Practicing

- As with the first three lessons, write the word KICK on the board. Fill in the phrases for each step: K—Knowing I'm Nervous, I—Irritating Thoughts, C—Calm Thoughts, and K—Keep Practicing. Point out that we practice facing fears by taking small steps. If we keep practicing with all of the small steps we set out for ourselves, soon we will be doing what we wanted to do all along, and with a lot more confidence.

- If there is time, review each step of the KICK plan. Point out that to make this plan work, the students should go in order, beginning with identifying their feelings of anxiety, then figuring out the nature of their irritating thoughts, then challenging those thoughts with calm thoughts, and, finally, making up a series of small steps to practice by using a feelings thermometer.

LESSON PLAN 10.4   (continued)
Homework Assignment

Explain the assignment:

> In order to help you practice with small steps, your homework assignment is to choose any false alarm type of anxiety that teens might face (asking someone out, public speaking, going on long trips away from family, and so on) and make up some small steps that a teen could use to build up to facing fears. Choose something interesting to you, and think of at least five small steps to build up to the real situation. Be sure to rate each step on the 0 to 10 feelings thermometer to show how someone would feel about each step before he or she had tried to face the fears. You can draw a picture to go with the small steps for extra credit.

Assessment

Note the students' ability to identify small steps that could be used to face specific feared situations. Repeat this lesson until accuracy is at 90 percent for students on the spectrum.

Social Skills Success for Students with Autism/Asperger's, copyright © 2011 John Wiley and Sons, Inc.

HANDOUT 10.3 Parent Information Letter About Anxiety Curriculum: Keep Practicing by Taking Small Steps

Dear Parents:

In our anxiety education lesson today, we focused on the concept of taking small steps to face fears. Adolescents benefit from trying out situations that trigger anxiety but are actually safe. Examples include giving speeches and speaking to other kids they don't know well. By taking small steps in doing what makes them nervous, adolescents can teach themselves that many situations that seem difficult are actually fun. Taking small steps to begin with, like giving a very short speech to a small group, can prevent panic reactions and help adolescents slowly build up their confidence. This ensures a smooth transition from an anxious to a more confident way of thinking and acting.

Once the general idea of taking small steps and practicing is mastered in one or two sample situations, students can often use this skill in a variety of other anxiety-producing situations. Adolescents can learn to face fear to fight fear.

Your child will be asked to practice taking some small steps in class and as part of homework on several occasions. These assignments will be individualized, and students will be encouraged to challenge themselves by finding a situation that causes them at least mild anxiety (such as trying a new activity they haven't done before but would like to start) and devising small steps to build up to facing the fear (like giving a practice speech in front of you and other family members).

As students practice with these small steps, it will be important for them to pay attention to generating calm thoughts to increase their confidence and reduce their anxiety. Studies have found that this is the best way for adolescents (in fact, people of all ages) to develop greater awareness of how emotions work and how to control anxiety effectively.

Sincerely,

LESSON PLAN 10.5 Skills Practice

SELECTED STUDENT NEED

- Learning how anxiety can be managed by using a coping plan (the KICK plan) and actively facing fears.

LEARNING OBJECTIVE

- Students will be able to face minor fears using the KICK plan.

STANDARDS AND BENCHMARKS

- Accurately verbalize the steps and meaning of the KICK plan.
- Use the KICK plan in facing fears in class and when needed in daily life.

MATERIALS AND RESOURCES

- Teen homework assignment from the previous lesson. Write the assignment on the board in advance, to be completed as part of students' class homework.
- Handout 10.4, "Parent Information Letter About Anxiety Curriculum: Using Incentives." This can be used in conjunction with working with parents of teens on the spectrum to help develop a home-based incentive program to increase a teen's motivation to face relevant fears and keep calm in class. This letter is meant to be tailored slightly to each individual family.

Introduction

In the skills practice phase, students are expected to master the meaning of the KICK plan and learn to use it in conjunction with taking small steps to face their fears. By practicing facing fears in small groups, they can attain peer support and modeling. Be careful to group the teen on the spectrum with sympathetic peers for this lesson. This lesson will generally be repeated up to six times, depending on available time and the needs of the student. More skills practice generally leads to better results for teens with significant anxiety issues.

This is also the time to implement a home–school incentive and information exchange program to help teens on the spectrum who have in-class meltdowns. This can be initiated with the sample parent letter (Handout 10.4). The letter describes a simple and highly effective means of daily communication between teacher and parents that lets parents provide motivating incentives to teens on a daily basis for keeping calm in class.

Before teaching the lesson, determine what fearful situation to have the class focus on for the day. Due to the multifaceted nature of anxiety and the need for repeated practice to achieve comfort with feared activities, choose class

Social Skills Success for Students with Autism/Asperger's, copyright © 2011 John Wiley and Sons, Inc.

LESSON PLAN 10.5 (continued)

activities that in some ways match the anxiety issues of the student on the autism spectrum. The following choices are good options for classroom-based practicing:

- *Giving speeches.* There are many ways of making this more and less anxiety provoking, which makes it ideally suited to practicing small steps and tailoring the activities to the anxiety level of students on the spectrum. To increase or decrease anxiety in a class speech, you can vary the topic (something interesting to the student versus boring; impersonal versus personal), size of the group watching the speech (from one person to the whole class), length of the speech, whether the student has note cards or is improvising, and whether the group is instructed to act receptive, natural, or intentionally inattentive (to simulate giving a speech under difficult conditions). The students could also be given the goal of making good eye contact with the group as a means of increasing the difficulty. Finally, students can add some intentional mistakes into their speeches to increase the difficulty. This can be a particularly powerful antidote to public speaking anxiety, because if a teen can survive making mistakes once, he will recognize that he could survive it again in future speeches, a liberating realization.

- *Acting out a skit.* To vary difficulty, students could either devise their own in class or act out a classic teen skit freely available on the Internet (see, for example, http://www.ultimatecampresource.com/site/camp-activities/camp-skits.html; http://usscouts.org/clipart/ScoutDoc/Skits/BBSkits.pdf). Taking a bigger role is going to be a bigger step in terms of facing fears for many teens. Many of the variables mentioned for speech-giving tasks can also be used to create multiple steps for this type of activity.

- *A performance of some kind: playing an instrument, singing, dancing, an art show, a stand-up comedy routine, and so on.* Again, multiple steps can be made by varying the difficulty level in terms of many of the same variables mentioned in the speech-giving tasks (for example, length of performance, size of audience, solo versus group presentation).

- *Small group disclosures of semipersonal topics.* Teens must agree to do this of their own free will so you may make it a choice for the day (and perhaps have other small groups working on speeches or other less personal activities). The ideal for this is that teens agree to provide a supportive listening environment for each person to disclose a past or existing fear. Then the group helps brainstorm on a KICK plan, emphasizing the calm thoughts and the small steps that the student might take to overcome it. Peer support for facing specific fears can be very helpful in some cases. Often it helps for the teacher to facilitate the small groups.

The Class Session

Start with, "Today we are going to review and practice using the KICK plan. When we use this plan to deal with false alarms if we feel anxious for no good reason, we can become more confident and take control of our emotions—not let them control us. We will continue to prove to ourselves that there is nothing to fear by trying things out gradually."

KICK Plan Review

- Review the KICK plan and discuss it in conjunction with a specific activity the class will practice in small groups today (see those listed in the lesson plan Introduction). Here are the steps:

  Step 1: K step. Focus on the physical cues of anxiety the teens might experience in the situation, such as tension. Emphasize that we all have our own way of noticing when we are feeling anxious.

  Step 2: I step. Review the irritating thoughts about the feared situation. Use the downward arrow technique from Lesson 10.2 to identify the most extreme, irrational aspects of these thoughts.

  Step 3: C step. Identify calm thoughts to counter each of the irritating thoughts. Teens need to use evidence to counter each irritating thought, focusing on either the likelihood that it would happen or whether it would be such a big deal if it did happen. If facing the fear seems safe, proceed to the next step.

  Step 4: K step. Devise small steps to practice to build up to fully facing a fear. Then start taking those steps slowly to gain confidence.

- In going through the KICK plan for the task of the day (say, giving speeches in small groups), be sure to point out that everyone will have irritating thoughts, calm thoughts, and set of small steps to practice. Encourage students to contribute some ideas about what irritating thoughts someone who was feeling anxiety about a situation might experience. Then ask students for help to develop possible calm thoughts and small steps for a person who is feeling nervous. Have each student write down his or her own personal KICK plan on a separate piece of paper. Encourage students to respect others' privacy with regard to this writing task and appropriately discipline students who violate this requirement. Students can do a downward arrow for their irritating thoughts, and then write the corresponding calm thoughts next to each irritating thought, as in the example given in Lesson 10.2. For the *keep practicing* step, students should write at least five steps that will build up to a reasonable level of difficulty for them personally (beginning with a step they would rate as a 0 and ending with a step they would rate as at least a 5 on the anxiety thermometer). Be sure they rate each step on the 0 to 10 scale (you may want to draw the feelings thermometer on the board the first few times you do this lesson plan).

- The first time you use this lesson plan with a given class, ask the students to reflect on what materials they will need to practice their small steps for the day (for example, something to read for a "speech"). For future skills practice lessons, assign this preparation of needed materials as part of the students' homework.

- Have students select a reasonable step from their list of small steps for themselves personally and assign the students into small groups (of whatever size fits your class environment—as few as two and up to ten students is fine) to begin practicing the step that each has selected.

- Help the student groups tailor their practicing to your goals for the day; for example, if you wanted students to practice making mistakes during speeches, ensure that the students brainstorm about what kinds of mistakes they might make. Being sensitive to students who need to take very small steps, emphasize that everyone is going at his or her own pace and students are allowed to choose as small a step as they need. For instance, if making mistakes was the goal, a very small step for some students might be to skip a single word in a paragraph they read to the group. A much larger step for many teens would be to mispronounce multiple words or repeatedly mispronounce a particular word in a peculiar way. The groups should be encouraged to be supportive, no matter what steps the group members choose to take.

- Generally each group member should have a chance to either repeat a step or go up another step or two in each class session. For instance, in giving speeches, often each group member might have two or three turns. Each student can decide whether to go up one step per turn or to stay at the same step throughout the class.

- Point out periodically to the students that the calm thoughts and small steps are slowly building up their confidence to do the given activities.

- Teachers should note that over the course of multiple sessions of skills practice, they should see the teen on the spectrum moving toward facing the higher steps on his list of small steps. Pay special attention

LESSON PLAN 10.5 (continued)

to his progress during skills practice and provide encouragement, support, and guidance as needed. If a student needs extra motivation, think of an incentive that might motivate him to put in more effort in facing fears during the skills practice lessons and negotiate this with him in private. It is helpful to ensure that the student remains in a small group with sympathetic peers while he is gaining confidence and to oversee the group dynamic to promote positive attitudes for his participation that will be conducive to successfully taking small steps.

Homework Assignment

Explain the assignment:

In order to help you practice with the KICK plan, your homework assignment is to choose any false alarm type of anxiety that teens can face (public speaking, going on long trips away from family, and so on), write a KICK plan for the situation like we did in class today, and then start taking some small steps outside class to build up to the real situation. Choose something interesting or worthwhile to you, and think of at least five small steps. Be sure to rate each step on the 0 to 10 feelings thermometer. Then take one or two steps and write a paragraph about what you did and how it went.

You may also want to contact the parent of the teen on the spectrum separately and suggest an area of anxiety to have the teen work on for the week and some sample small steps, relevant to the teen's most significant areas of anxiety: social, generalized, or separation. If the teen has social anxiety, perhaps small steps with social encounters in the community or neighborhood could be tried. For generalized anxiety, making minor mistakes on purpose relevant to the teen's specific concerns can be helpful. For separation anxiety, being away from parents in ways that challenge the teen are helpful to practice. Of course, like everyone else, teens on the spectrum need to make a KICK plan for whatever homework task is selected; and, they need to have some say in what fears to face to keep their interest and motivation up.

Assessment

Note the students' ability to take small steps that could be used to face feared situations. Repeat this lesson until accuracy is at 90 percent for students on the spectrum.

Social Skills Success for Students with Autism/Asperger's, copyright © 2011 John Wiley and Sons, Inc.

HANDOUT 10.4 Parent Information Letter About Anxiety Curriculum: Using Incentives

Dear Parents:

We have begun the skills practice phase of our anxiety program, and this involves using a coping strategy called the KICK plan when facing fears. Your child will be given homework to face specific fears tailored to his or her anxiety issues that we assessed using questionnaires several weeks ago. For your child, we will specifically focus on [DESCRIBE]. To practice overcoming this, he or she will take small steps doing things like practicing giving speeches to family members, making and receiving phone calls, talking to store clerks and waiters, and saying hello to neighbors. I will try to contact you to brainstorm with you on the specifics of what to begin with for your child. Then your child will have a homework assignment to make a KICK plan for the situation, think of some small steps to take to face the situation, and to try out some of these steps during the week—for example, giving a few practice speeches to you and the family.

Once the steps to be taken have been determined with your child's active involvement, he or she may need to be motivated with some incentives to actually take the steps. This is perfectly fine. Once fears are overcome, you don't need to give incentives anymore, since adolescents are naturally motivated to do things once they are no longer afraid. So this will be a short-term addition. For each step your child takes, offer the incentive. Don't give it unless he or she takes the step. And don't renegotiate any deals you've made once your child has agreed to the terms.

Examples of incentives are a small amount of money (whatever is appropriate in your family), extra time using electronic devices (you have to be able to restrict your child's use of this in the first place if this is going to be effective), and small treats. It is most important that your child is actually motivated by the incentive.

I also would like to set up a separate incentive program with you to help your child stay calm in class. For your child, it will be helpful to define what we mean by keeping calm. For him or her, it will be [DESCRIBE], and finding a quiet place to recover his or her composure. I would be glad to send you a very brief daily e-mail or text message to let you know if he or she kept calm in class each day. This could be one of the requirements for your child to earn the daily incentive that you set up with him or her for working on the small steps and facing fears tasks.

Sincerely,

CHAPTER 11

Preventing and Dealing with Victimization

"In middle school, I went from a school of five hundred to a school of seventeen hundred. I was overwhelmed. I just kept to myself. I never used my locker, just kept my coat on all day and carried my gym stuff around with me in a large duffel bag. I was an easy target for kids who wanted to pick on someone. I was tripped in the hallway while others laughed. There were one or two kids who would put a little drop of mustard on my nice white shirt (which I liked to wear every day). This upset me greatly, so I got upset and I got into trouble. Being bullied put me on a path that lasted my entire middle and high school career. I moved from someone who scored all A's to someone skipping thirty-five days a semester and never getting higher than a D."

The major focus of this chapter is exploring effective approaches to address bullying with special considerations for tweens and teens on the spectrum. Effective approaches require whole-school interventions. We first review what we know about other common forms of victimization: teasing and highly aggressive boys we will call "frequent fighters." Then we review the two main forms of bullying and how to deal with them.

Types of Victimization

We are going to divide victimization into four types, based on the most effective strategies to deal with each: teasing, physical aggression, face-to-face bullying, and cyberbullying. Knowing the type of victimization teens experience and the types of responses that lead to successful versus unsuccessful outcomes is important for determining which response is best for each type of victimization.

Teasing

Most victimization involves teasing. Research studies have found that teasing reaches a peak in middle school, with some teasers and teased pupils in every classroom. Perpetrators are motivated to tease by the pleasure they get at seeing their victim react poorly. Teasing may be humorous, but the humor is at the expense of the victim. Teasing is frequently done in front of bystanders.

Rude negative feedback may be confused with teasing but actually is not. An example of rude feedback is when a teen says to another "You stink!" This may be a tease, totally unfounded on any characteristics of the victim, or it may indicate that the receiver of this information is playing with a group of peers that are much better than he is at the game they are playing and they feel he is making their side do poorly at the game. This statement may also be pointing out poor hygiene or poor personal habits. If the statement turns out to be rude negative feedback, then the best course of action is for the receiver to improve his hygiene or to play with others closer to his skill level.

EFFECTIVE RESPONSES TO BEING TEASED

One study had children between eight and eleven years old view videos of a child being teased by two other children. The victim responded either with humor, by ignoring, or with hostility (for instance, teasing back). The children viewing the videos rated the humorous response as the most effective, followed by ignoring, and the hostile response as least effective. Furthermore, the victim's response to teasing significantly affected the viewer's perceptions of the friendliness and popularity of the victim. Victims using the humorous responses were rated as most popular. Thus, humorous responses to being teased can improve a kid's reputation. Both the PEERS intervention and Children's Friendship Training teach students to use humorous comebacks to being teased (making fun of the perpetrator's inability to tease well). The evidence has been clear that students on the spectrum can be taught to decrease this form of victimization on their own. They can be trained to use a few funny comebacks (sidestepping their poor humor abilities), which will handle most forms of teasing.

Physical Aggression

We distinguish between frequent fighters, who are nonselective in their targets and generally aggressive, and bullies, who are very selective in their targets and not generally aggressive. Unlike bullies, frequent fighters have had a long history of aggressive behavior, usually starting in elementary school. Some begin to get into trouble with the law as they grow older. Frequent fighters are not liked by peers. Studies that have explored the backgrounds of these boys found that from very young ages, their parents tended to have poor control over them and allowed them to spend large parts of their after-school time unsupervised. Many have poor grades, and some may have learning disabilities.

Starting in late elementary school, these aggressive boys are likely to form relationships with other frequent fighters. These don't seem to be true friendships but more friends of convenience. Such children, if left to associate with other highly aggressive children, have a high risk for juvenile delinquency by their teen years.

EFFECTIVE APPROACHES TO FREQUENT FIGHTING

Some frequent fighters are diagnosable with attention deficit hyperactivity disorder. Effective intervention during the elementary school years typically is a combination of stimulant medication and teaching parents more effective parenting skills. This combined treatment can have a substantial impact on these children if the parents can participate fully. However, the older the student gets before beginning these treatments, the less likely the treatments will help, especially after these young people start to hang out with others like themselves. Traditional forms of treatment have not been effective. Frequent fighters don't respond to individual counseling. And one study found that group treatment of these teens can actually increase their antisocial behavior because they are prone to communicate antisocial behaviors to other like-minded members of the group.

Thus, in the absence of effective therapeutic approaches, schools often resort to a zero tolerance approach where these adolescents are placed in alternative schools, mainly to protect the rest of the students. In addition, kids on the spectrum can be taught to avoid frequent fighters (since they don't select their targets but fight with whomever happens to be nearby). Lesson Plan 11.1 addresses this. Peer mentors (see Chapter Twelve) can also play a role in teaching students on the spectrum how to avoid frequent fighters by avoiding where they hang out.

Bullying

Bullying involves an imbalance of physical, social, or emotional power between the victim and the perpetrator. It is defined as repeated (once per week or more) attempts to intimidate or inflict unprovoked injury or discomfort on the same victim by one or more specific other peers. The intent is to cause emotional or physical harm to the victim. Bullying can continue over the course of days, months, or even years. The victim is left traumatized, while the bully shows a lack of concern and compassion.

Victimization is a prevalent problem for teens. Overall, 30.9 percent of middle school students reported being victimized three or more times in the past year and 7.4 percent reported being bullied. The prevalence for teens on the spectrum is much greater—perhaps as high as 75 percent for being bullied.

We draw the distinction between classic, face-to-face bullying, which we will refer to simply as bullying, and cyberbullying, which we discuss in the next section.

Bullying, while present in elementary school, becomes a major problem affecting more students starting in middle school. Most frequent locations are going to and from school, including the school bus; in bathrooms; and in poorly supervised areas of the schoolyard. The bully always has significantly more power than the victim in face-to-face bullying. This power may come from the bully's physical strength or with the help of a group of friends of the bully (referred to as passive bullies) who assist in bullying. Effective intervention strategies must include disbanding this bullying group, since it is a source of social support for bullying activities.

Unlike frequent fighters, bullies may be well regarded by teachers and supervisors, or at least not distinguished as troublemakers. Individual risk factors for bullying for boys include an impulsive, dominant personality; a lack of empathy; positive attitudes toward violence; and above-average physical strength. Unlike frequent fighters who will fight anywhere, bullies have to feel that no one is watching or no one who is watching will intervene.

Although bullying is usually done out of sight of teachers and adult supervisors, other students may be present. Some of these students form the bully group and either take part or encourage the victimization. Others participate due to peer pressure. Still others are bystanders who happen to be present when an individual act takes place.

Bystanders are affected in different ways. Some may feel distress in witnessing the torment of peers and may be anxious at the prospect of being a future target. Some fear associating with victims because of possible retaliation, and some may be afraid of lowering their own social standing by associating with victims. These students often feel guilty for not doing more to help victims but are afraid to report incidents. Bystanders may feel unsafe and powerless to take action; they don't think they can do it anonymously and don't think the adults will take any effective action.

OSTRACISM

In much of the writing about bullying, ostracism has been considered part of victimization. However, the term refers to a broad range of behavior, only part of which meets criteria for victimization. The threat of or actual ostracism, when used as a control technique by a dominant teen (usually a girl who is dominant in a small clique of girls), is a form of bullying referred to as relational aggression. There is one intensive study showing how a dominant girl kept other girls in her clique in line with the threat of ostracism if they became more popular or didn't do what she wanted them to do. Two elements distinguish this type of ostracism: it is used to intimidate and is initiated by one or a few members who are able to get others (usually with the same implied threat) to go along. Long-term follow-up studies of girls who use relational aggression indicate a poor outcome in many ways similar to those of frequent fighters.

Another type of ostracism is not bullying; rather it results from the problematic social behavior of an individual. In Chapter Two, we discussed a method that developmental psychologists use to assess how much peers like to socialize or work with an individual student. They ask each student in private how much, on a scale of 1 to 5, they would like to work with or socialize with each other student in their class. The researchers can then categorize students in terms of peer acceptance using this method. Three main categories concern us. Some students have high ratings on the "liked" scale by several or all of the other students, but no one rates them as above 1 on the "disliked" scale. These are popular, or "accepted," students. Other students are not rated above 1 on either the "liked" or "disliked" scales. These students are "overlooked" by peers. Then there are students who have high ratings on the "disliked" scale by most or all of the peer group and high ratings on the "liked" scale by no one. These students are ostracized. One study found that when a student who was ostracized was placed together to play with two other students who didn't know him, these new peers also disliked him within forty-five minutes of play. It was the social behaviors that these ostracized students brought with them to social situations that were responsible for this peer reaction. They were bossy, intrusive, poor sports in games, and frustrating to socialize with. The best approach to help these ostracized students is to teach them better social skills so that interacting with them becomes a pleasant experience. This is the focus of the PEERS intervention and Children's Friendship Training.

TEENS WITH AUTISM SPECTRUM DISORDERS AS VICTIMS

Students with autism spectrum disorders are usually ostracized by their classmates. We have seen throughout this book that very few teens on the spectrum have friends, let alone close friends. Studies show that teens who are liked less (and disliked more) are more likely to be victimized. About 75 percent of children and adolescents with autism spectrum disorders have been bullied, most commonly face-to-face bullying.

In one instance, a bully would sit behind a teen on the spectrum in a class and start flicking him in the ear and putting eraser shavings on his head. Out of class, the bully and his bully ring would shove the student into the hall lockers. Another example concerned a bathroom that had been taken over by a group of frequent fighters. Neurotypical students knew to stay away from this bathroom. However, one teen on the spectrum was unaware of this danger and was beaten up as he entered the bathroom.

Kids with a desire to bully scout out potential victims they think will be fun to torture. Adolescents on the spectrum are selected because they appear weak and seem to be good prey. Students on the autism spectrum are especially prone to being victimized for three reasons. First, they are easy targets for perpetrators. They have not developed the tough social veneer of others their age, they wear their hearts on their sleeves, and they don't try to hide the fact that they are upset. Second, they have not learned to avoid situations that present risk of victimization. Third, they often have a negative reputation with peers and school personnel. Thus, bystanders may be less inclined to report bullying and school personnel may have a hard time believing any charges that a teen on the spectrum makes against a bully.

Other forms of bullying may be less obvious to school personnel unfamiliar with characteristics of autism spectrum disorders. Strongly obsessive behaviors can make teens on the spectrum easy targets. Bullies quickly learn what buttons they need to press to trigger an outburst. The bullies manipulate the teen into disruptive behavior and then watch their victim get into trouble for behavior they triggered. For example, one teen had an obsession about sitting on the same seat of the school bus every day. A bully, after seeing this obsessive behavior, decided that this was going to be his seat. The teen on the spectrum became so upset that the bus driver complained about him and refused to take him on the bus.

Some bullying results from unintentional provocations by teens on the spectrum. An example is when a kid on the spectrum attempts to fit in with a crowd that does not want to accept him. He fails to perceive the subtle forms of rejection he gets at first in these attempts, so he may keep on trying. (Chapters Five and Seven address this problem.) Eventually more poorly behaved members of the crowd start to physically intimidate the teen. The intimidation may last beyond the point at which the teen stops attempting to join the crowd. In one case, a thirteen-year-old girl on the spectrum attempted to join the popular crowd. Her numerous attempts at first were mildly rebuffed (with lots of eye rolling), but she persisted. The rebuffs became stronger, and eventually some of the girls started physically assaulting her.

Teens on the spectrum are often sticklers for enforcing school rules. They are more likely to report minor infractions that most students let slide, and this may get them into trouble with the other students. For example, one teen with autism spectrum disorder was encouraged by school administrators to report other teens who bullied him. At first he reported others who were making threatening statements. Eventually he reported teens who were committing minor infractions of school rules, so that his reports became a daily occurrence. This angered his fellow students and set him apart even more.

Cyberbullying

Although most bullying is the face-to-face variety, bullying may also occur in cyberspace: by phone, text messaging, picture and video clips, e-mail, chatroom, instant messaging, and over Web sites. Cyberbullying can involve threatening messages to individuals in the form of harassment, put-downs, stalking, and death threats. Here are some examples from the news media:

- After a quarrel with his girlfriend, a boy photo-edited her face onto a pornographic photo and distributed the photo to all of his friends and acquaintances.

- A fifteen-year-old boy was humiliated when a film he made of himself emulating a *Star Wars* fight scene was posted on the Internet by some classmates.

- Cell phone pictures of an overweight boy, secretly taken of him in the locker room, were distributed to many of his classmates.

- Web sites were set up to circulate rumors or ask students to vote on the ugliest or fattest kid in school.

Cyberbullies feel that they can't be detected or, if detected, that they can get away with their behavior without being punished. Techniques such as temporary e-mail accounts and pay-as-you-go cell phones are readily available to justify this feeling. Cyberbullying most often occurs outside school hours using home computers (except for cyberbullying by text messaging). School officials are often reluctant to take action against students who make posts to Web sites while they are not in school. The anonymity of the Internet and knowing that they are less likely to be punished for acts taking place off school grounds makes cyberbullying more attractive.

Perhaps the most accurate estimates of the prevalence of cyberbullying come from studies using anonymous disclosure by the students. One study claimed that one in four teens has been a cybervictim. Another study found that 11 percent were victims of cyberbullying, 7 percent were bullies and victims, and 4 percent were bullies. When students were asked how long each type of cyberbullying had lasted, 56.5 percent said it had lasted one or two weeks, 18.8 percent said about a month, 5.8 percent replied about six months, 8.7 percent said about a year, and 10.1 percent said it had gone on for more than a year. Summing together reports of persistence for a month or longer, which would meet the criterion for bullying as continued victimization, about 43.4 percent of victims of cyberattacks were chronically bullied. But 56.5 percent of victims had short-lived experiences. This is an important statistic to consider when advising students on the best responses to cyberbullying because the responses of these students may have shortened their victimization.

While face-to-face bullying involves a power imbalance, cyberbullying supposedly does not because social status and physical strength do not matter. This difference might lead those who would not normally bully to try cyberbullying. However, at least one study does not support this, as many cybervictims also reported being traditional victims, and most cyberbullies were also face-to-face bullies. Also similar to face-to-face bullying, boys were more likely to be cyberbullies than girls.

Only 8.5 percent of students who were cybervictims said they reported cyberbullying to the adults at school. The low reporting rates probably are due to the perception that school officials will not take any effective action, rather than reflecting the actual incidence of bullying during school hours. Cyberbullying frequently takes the form of text messaging over cell phones. (Although carrying a working cell phone is against school policy for most middle schools, this policy is difficult to enforce. The majority of students in one survey admitted using their cell phone during the school day.) Only 15.5 percent of students reported cyberbullying to parents, with girls more likely to tell parents than boys were. Reports to parents were low because teens said they feared the loss of online privileges.

CYBERBULLYING AND KIDS ON THE SPECTRUM

Although students with autism spectrum disorders are more likely to tell parents about bullying and cyberbullying, there have been some tragic cases where they did not. Thus, parents of teens on the spectrum are not safe in assuming that they will know if cyberbullying is happening to their teen.

LEGAL ISSUES.   School officials have both greater and lesser investigative authority than the police have over students when incidents happen on school grounds. Though police officers need probable cause and a warrant to search a student's locker or backpack, school administrators may need only reasonable suspicion that a school rule has been violated. In terms of investigating incidents of victimization, it seems that school officials are on safer ground with face-to-face bullying since the impact on the school environment is obvious.

Cyberbullying is another matter. At the time of writing in 2011, much of the legal groundwork has yet to be laid due to the new and constantly changing technology. Some of the problems that school officials encounter in trying to intervene in cases of cyberbullying can be resolved through well-thought-out legislation. Other problems have to do with freedom-of-speech issues. Still other problems are related to the reach of school officials to intervene on behavior that occurs after school and off campus where and when cyberbullying can occur.

Looking at the cell phone of a teen who has been accused of bullying may not be within a school's investigative authority. If the complaining student has saved the threatening message, administrators may be on firmer ground. But in this case, the evidence is sufficient without looking at the perpetrator's phone.

Taking action against a student for off-campus behavior or not during regular school hours may also be a legal gray area. One Web site suggests that crafting consents that parents and students sign upon being enrolled at school may be a way around this. This consent covers what is and is not acceptable use for on-campus use of school technology. It may include a provision that covers dangerous or abusive actions by a student that directly affects another student, the school itself, its staff, or the educational environment, allowing the school to take action in these cases. Schools are advised to have attorneys craft these policies and consent documents.

LEGISLATION.   Forty-three states had bullying prevention laws as of June 2010. At least twenty-one states have legislation against cyberbullying: Arkansas, California, Delaware, Florida, Georgia, Idaho, Iowa, Kansas, Maryland, Minnesota, Missouri, Nebraska, New Hampshire, New Jersey, North Carolina, Oklahoma, Oregon, Pennsylvania, Rhode Island, South Carolina, and Washington. Bullypolice.org provides an update on state laws.

There are many issues with these laws. Many statutes fail to define bullying, leaving it unclear whether their provisions apply only to physical bullying or to threat, humiliation, and intimidation. Laws that do define bullying frequently are inconsistent. Some states say that school conduct codes must explicitly prohibit cyberbullying even if it does not take place on school campuses; some states explicitly exclude it. Many state antibullying laws require schools to develop policies against bullying, have educational programs, and establish reporting procedures. The bullying laws of Connecticut, New Hampshire, New Jersey, New York, Washington, and West Virginia include provisions that either mandate or encourage individuals to report school bullying incidents to authorities. However, there is little agreement about the reporting threshold for bullying in terms of frequency, duration, or seriousness of the bullying that would trigger filing a report.

INEFFECTIVE SCHOOL INTERVENTIONS

Reporting bullying alone (without any further intervention) even with awareness-raising efforts (such as educating students as to why bullying is wrong) do little to reduce the frequency and nature of bullying. Studies show that the strategies students perceive as least effective are those that only involve rules against cyberbullying or telling them not to bully.

Anger management classes and self-esteem sessions are sometimes used as interventions for teens identified as bullies. This approach is based on misconceptions about characteristics and motivations of teens who bully and are likely to be ineffective. Anger is not a primary motivating factor for most teens who bully. Furthermore, studies show that the self-esteem of bullies is not noticeably different from the self-esteem of students who don't bully. Rather, it is the self-esteem of the victims that is impaired by being bullied and is a contributing factor to their victimization.

Similar to the effects on frequent fighters, there is evidence that treating bullies in group therapy provides them with other bullies as role models and social support for future bullying. Even more ill advised is to have bullies and victims in the same group. Bullying is not a misunderstanding between two children, but predatory behavior by someone who has a power advantage over someone else. For this reason, mediation and conflict resolution techniques, which are common and reasonable strategies school personnel use to resolve conflicts between peers of relatively equal power, are not appropriate to use for victims and bullies. They also may further victimize a kid who has been bullied because of the power imbalance of one of the negotiating parties.

It has become popular to target bystanders as potential sources for help in preventing and decreasing bullying. Many urge students in general not to be bystanders but to report bullying. However, as yet, there are no documented cases where this has been an effective intervention strategy. Employing bystanders to inform on bullies is unlikely to work, as school officials currently do not have a reputation among students of following up on reports or having decisive interventions to deal with bullies. If adults do not set the tone by intervening decisively to address bullying, student bystanders will assume that adults either are unconcerned or are powerless to change bullies' behaviors. Bystanders must see the adults in action first before risking themselves and their standing in school to report bullying incidences. They can't be the front line of a bullying intervention because the power imbalance potentially applies to them in the same way as the victims.

Zero tolerance or three-strikes policies for physical bullying are mandated in Georgia and a number of local communities. These consequences may be appropriate when a frequent fighter poses a danger to the student community through his aggressiveness. However, harsh consequences such as these have the unintended consequence of discouraging reporting of suspected bullying by bystanders and adults who may have difficulty justifying the severity of response after they report a bully.

Effective Ways of Handling Bullying

Before describing steps to setting up an effective antibullying program, we first describe two approaches that can more directly help teens on the spectrum: teaching safety and measures that improve his reputation among his peers. We also describe an informal approach for administrators that can head off continuing bullying.

Teaching Safety

Since beginning middle school students are particularly vulnerable to victimization by older students, times and areas for activities such as lunch and physical education that are separate from those for other grades should be considered. The younger grade could be assigned its own area, with a large "no-man's-land" between areas so that straying students can be easily detected.

Kids on the autism spectrum need to be taught how to stay safe. They need to be explicitly taught how to avoid the more dangerous places and people on the school campus as well as in the local community. They need to be taught not to personally challenge rule violations of others such as highly aggressive teens. They should avoid being the rules police. If an aggressive teen cuts in front of them in line, rather than standing up for the rule that "no one cuts in line," they need to be quiet and let it slide. This is a skill that most neurotypical adolescents have mastered. This skill can be addressed within a mentorship relationship, such as that outlined in Chapter Twelve. It is also addressed in Lesson Plan 11.1.

Improving Reputation Among Peers

Many students on the spectrum have developed a negative reputation among their peers. When bullying starts, they are less likely to have someone come to their aid, less likely to have a bystander report the incident, and less likely to have a best friend who can lessen the impact of bullying. Many of the chapters in this book address skills that will help improve this reputation and make the teen more accepted among the general peer group in terms of "like to work with" ratings. Chapter Four helps teens expand interests so as to be seen as more intellectually competent among peers. Chapters Six and Seven improve the conversational skills necessary to work with and seem friendly to peers. The older peer mentor described in Chapter Twelve may help peer acceptance further by specific coaching to promote the teen fitting in. Chapter Ten focuses on eliminating anxiety-related responses that may stigmatize the teen.

Having a best friend protects against victimization. It is harder for a bully to victimize a teen who is usually with a best friend (plus there is a witness who might report the incident). Thus, social skills interventions that increase peer liking and promote best friendships may also protect against victimization. In order to help teens avoid selecting the wrong crowd to approach, social skills curricula should include modules teaching teens how to select a crowd that is likely to accept them, how to look for feedback on whether their attempted entry into this crowd has been accepted or turned down, and how to make a graceful exit if they are turned down. These are elements of the PEERS program. Teacher help in selecting a suitable crowd is addressed in Chapter Eight.

INEFFECTIVE AND EFFECTIVE BULLYING INTERVENTIONS

ANTIBULLYING INTERVENTIONS THAT ARE NOT LIKELY TO WORK

- Telling students not to bully
- Making rules against bullying without any further intervention
- Anger management classes and self-esteem enhancement sessions for adolescents identified as bullies
- Treating bullies in group therapy with other bullies or with their victims in the same group
- Mediation and conflict resolution efforts between victims and bullies
- Trying to get bystanders to inform on bullies without having a track record for effective intervention
- Zero tolerance or three-strikes policies

INTERVENTIONS THAT WORK

- Teaching kids on the spectrum explicitly how to stay safe from the more dangerous places and people on the school campus as well as in the local community
- Working to improve the student's reputation among peers
- Helping the student develop closer friendships
- Teachers and supervisors intervening immediately in any bullying situation—even if there's only a suspicion that bullying may be taking place

Informal Approaches to Head Off Continuing Bullying

The crux of any effective antibullying program is teachers' and supervisors' willingness to become immediately involved in stopping this problem. Failing to act when teachers observe bullying is equivalent to tacit support. Leaving students unsupervised fails to protect victims from bullies. Actions early in a bullying situation that just started can be more effective than the same actions after bullying has gone on for a while. If it is left unchecked, a sense of entitlement develops in the bully when he has been getting away with victimizing for a while.

Rather than waiting for the evidence to build up against a particular teen and having to take more severe measures, bullying caught at the start may require only an informal meeting with the principal and a warning that the alleged bully will be under observation (together with a means to implement this). The amount of evidence need not be great, as it is approached informally and only as a suspicion. The purpose of the meeting is framed as "keeping the teen out of trouble." In many cases, this will act as an effective deterrent. If not, documenting this discussion and describing this approach is often helpful, as when parents are later called in if the incidents continue. The next sections describe a more formal comprehensive program to address bullying.

STEP 1: MAKING INITIAL ASSESSMENTS

Effective antibullying programs should always start with anonymous surveys of teachers, students, and school staff. Web sites such as Survey Monkey allow keeping track of who completes the survey without linking the survey responses to them. Thus, administrators can require everyone to complete their survey anonymously to get a more accurate picture.

It should be up to staff and teachers where they complete their own survey (at home or school). But students should complete the survey in the privacy of their own home to deter intrusion or coercion by other students.

The teacher assessment should start off by including any relevant state laws and school board statutes regarding bullying. It should include open-ended questions about teacher attitudes and beliefs about their roles in antibullying programs. It is also helpful to have teachers list trouble spots on the school campus that they think should be addressed by an antibullying program. It also should include suggestions about what is needed in order to strengthen their roles to enforce antibullying policies and statutes, given that they are busy fulfilling their educational missions. Having teachers suggest how they can accomplish all of their regularly assigned duties and yet work in supervision of hot-spot areas for bullying is often helpful. A separate survey should be addressed to other school staff members such as resource officers, school nurses, food service employees, school bus drivers, and anyone else who may be present when bullying incidents occur. After this information is gathered, an initial meeting should be set up with teachers to work out the details of how the program should be implemented.

Since anonymous student questionnaires are the most accurate means to assess the frequency and location of bullying, the student questionnaire is vital in determining the needs of the school. This is the best way to get bystanders involved so that they don't risk being victims themselves. The questionnaire should first have definitions of bullying and cyberbullying and then have multiple-choice questions asking about different types of bullying and cyberbullying and how often they have occurred to that student. This is to be used in subsequent evaluations of the effectiveness of any program that the school designs. If repeat questionnaire frequencies decrease, then you are on the correct path.

Another section of the questionnaire should contain questions regarding how often students have observed each type of bullying and cyberbullying. Open-ended questions should have students report different times and locations that they have observed bullying. This will serve as a guide to deploy supervisors. These should also include dangerous places in and around the school campus, because these locations will be used in Lesson Plan 11.1 to teach safety to students on the spectrum. Other open-ended questions should include the kinds of strategies that students have found helpful in stopping and preventing bullying. A final open-ended question would ask students for suggestions as to the kind of help and education they would like in order to help them address bullying and cyberbullying.

STEP 2: INSTITUTING SCHOOL CODES

Most schools have rules or regulations prohibiting the use of cell phones during school hours. Most students report that they disregard these regulations, and cell phone use, particularly texting, is widespread. Similarly, any codes or rules addressing bullying will have minimal effect by themselves in changing student behavior or the school climate regarding victimization. However, such codes will serve as a precondition for enforcement. School rules should be directed toward the bully or fighter and those who may be incited to bully or spread rumors. It should also plainly list enforceable consequences of violations in specific terms.

Our experience with codifying rules suggests that things never work out perfectly as intended. Therefore, formulation of rules should be a continuous process with a first attempt and then a later evaluation to see if the rules had the intended impact. A particularly good set of rules would have the following features:

- Clearly defined specific bullying behaviors graded in terms of severity.

- Clearly defined consequences that are graduated to fit the offenses. The initial consequences should not be so severe that people will be hesitant to report bullies.

- Less severe consequences for first documented offenses. Examples of good consequences are "restraining orders" (the bully is not allowed within one hundred feet of the victim for any reason), detention (which should not be with a group of other bullies), and conferences with parents of teens who are caught bullying. For any damage or loss incurred by the victim, monetary restitution without face-to face contact with the victim would be an additional consequence.

- Parents of identified bullies should be informed that they will be required to meet with the school principal to inform them of the incident and consequences.

- Parents of victims should be informed of the action against the bully. They should be told they will be contacted discretely and confidentially to avoid public embarrassment of the vulnerable victim (who may not have told them about the bullying). In cases of severe bullying, individual psychotherapy should be recommended for the victim.

STEP 3: SETTING UP REPORTING PROCEDURES

Most of the burden of detection of rule violations should be with the adults rather than with teens to inform on each other. Bully reporting by students should be confidential but not anonymous because anonymous reports invite abuse, particularly by bullies. Online reporting forms have the virtue of increased confidentiality since no other students will see the student making the report. There should also be a report booklet for teachers kept in a central secure place in the school, so that when someone makes a report on a particular student, teachers can immediately see what other reports have been made on that student and act accordingly. The reports should address even a suspicion of bullying and not be included in the student's official record. This also includes any informal meetings between the principal and student described above. The lower standard for reporting will serve to encourage more disclosure, since there may not be consequences if further investigation determines otherwise. Yard and lunchroom supervisors should report all incidents and should not accept the victim's word that everything was in fun.

Thus, if a bully–victim pattern emerges, schools have the evidence to pursue immediate action.

STEP 4: SETTING UP MONITORING AND SUPERVISION OF IDENTIFIED HOT SPOTS

The completed surveys described in step 1 should be used to modify supervision practices. Hot spots identified by student and teacher surveys should be included in monitoring efforts. Only adults who are willing and feel capable of intervening in bullying situations should be assigned to these key areas. The teacher survey should provide valuable information on the level of commitment of teachers and suggestions on how to accomplish the additional supervision required by antibullying programs.

Some hot spots lend themselves more to the installation of security cameras rather than a live supervisor. A prime example is the school bus. School bus drivers have traffic safety as their first priority and can't be monitoring their passengers. Procedures should be developed if a violent incident occurs on the bus. The bus driver should be given resources and procedures to call for help.

STEP 5: CRAFTING AND DISTRIBUTING CONSENT LETTERS TO PARENTS AND STUDENTS

Many schools have parents and students sign a document agreeing to abide by school rules. This document may also serve as a deterrent to litigious parents when it is crafted with legal advice. If school personnel have to enforce sanctions against a bully, they will be on firmer legal ground with a no-bullying policy that the alleged bully and his parents have previously signed. Because of the variation in the laws of each state, the policies of each school district, and the state of flux in legal precedents, we cannot provide a sample consent letter, only outline possible content.

The consent form should be part of a parent letter that describes the following details of the antibullying program:

- Applicable school codes and rules
- Acceptable-use policies for on-campus use of school technology
- A provision that covers dangerous or abusive actions by a student that directly affects another student, the school itself, staff, or the educational environment and allows the school to take action in these cases

- Reporting procedures and guidelines for gathering evidence by parents who wish to lodge a complaint
- Consequences for the student caught bullying

Effective Ways of Handling Cyberbullying

The fact that 56.5 percent of victims had short-lived experiences of being cyberbullied means that many students were able to handle the incidents themselves. Studies report that students are able to suggest some basic strategies for effectively dealing with cyberbullying, but were less likely to be aware of strategies to request the removal of objectionable Web sites. Handout 11.1 addresses this need. Teens report the most effective strategies to be blocking people online who bully and refusing to pass along cyberbullying messages. They also list complaining to moderators of online groups, who can block offensive messages.

There is a lot to be said for instructing teens on how to deal with cyberbullying. First, it may be effective in cutting off bullying by e-mail, instant messaging, and text messaging that involve contact between only bully and victim. Second, it is an important life skill to learn. However, it is not effective for many forms of bullying, as the following examples show.

- Determined school administrators and parents can, with the help of district attorneys and news media, shut down offensive Web sites even when the Webmaster has initially been unresponsive. One Web site was set up as a gossip site in which students could report anything they wanted about other students. There was no effective monitoring of content. Many of the postings were harmless, but hundreds of other conversations were filled with racial slurs, name-calling, and extremely hurtful language. One targeted group was the African American Awareness Club. Many of these negative postings were aimed at members of this group. Postings also included tasteless and offensive "jokes" about slavery and the Ku Klux Klan. This caused substantial disruption of the school. Angry parents and a school principal enlisted the aid of the media. The Web site eventually ceased operations.
- Virtual polling sites can also be used to promote bullying. A virtual poll called "The Interschool Ho" was created to "rate" 150 students.

When parents and teachers became aware of this activity, they contacted the Webmaster by e-mail to close down the site. That action was futile. Only a phone call from the city district attorney finally persuaded the Webmaster to remove the offensive site. The site no longer exists.

- One girl videotaped friends at a café. She egged them on as they laughed and made mean-spirited, sexual comments about another eighth-grade girl, and she posted the video on YouTube. When school administrators discovered the video, they suspended her for two days. The suspended girl's father, an attorney, sued the school. The courts initially sided against school administrators since they couldn't make a strong enough case that the students' actions disrupted the operation of the school.

Lesson Plan 11.1 emphasizes what the teens on the spectrum can and should do to stay out of harm's way. The parent is used as a conduit for the student's reports of bullying in order to ensure that students on the spectrum are reporting appropriate offenses. Handout 11.1 also lists courses of action against cyberbullying.

LESSON PLAN 11.1 Protecting Yourself from Bullies

SELECTED STUDENT NEED

- Most students with autism spectrum disorders have been victims of bullying. Protecting oneself from cyberbullying requires a skill set that students can learn. Without specific training, they are extremely vulnerable to this predatory behavior.

LEARNING OBJECTIVES

- Students will learn how to respond to milder forms of cyberbullying so that it is not likely to continue.
- Students will learn to avoid situations that could lead to bullying.
- Students will learn how to enlist their parents in helping them stop bullying

STANDARD AND BENCHMARK

- Notice students demonstrating understanding of the approaches in this lesson through appropriate responses to questions posed.

MATERIALS AND RESOURCES

- Results of online questionnaires will help teachers determine the rates of different forms of bullying and dangerous locations for students in and around campus. This information specific to the school campus can be added to this lesson plan. Send Handout 11.1 home to parents prior to the lesson and have a copy for teens to review as part of the lesson.

Introduction

This lesson focuses on what students and their parents can do to prevent or stop bullying and cyberbullying.

The Class Session

Begin, "Today you are going to learn about how to protect yourself from dangerous situations and keep yourself safe from bullies and mean people." Then continue to these topics:

1. *Describe how to avoid calling the attention of bullies.* Take the largest student in the class aside and tell him to act tough and cut in line in front of you without asking. Now tell the class, "Suppose you are waiting in line with several other teens to get into a movie and someone cuts in line in front of you like this. I want you to tell me what's wrong with reacting this way." [Motion to your confederate to cut in line.] "Hey

you're not supposed to do that. Don't you know there is no cutting in line? I'm going to tell the manager!" Now ask what's wrong with this response. Accept that it's not your job to point out rule violations. Ask, "What could happen to you if you did this to a bully? Accept that he may hurt or threaten you and may start looking for you when he sees you and make trouble and start picking on you. The moral of this story is, Don't try to be the rules police with bullies."

2. *Teach staying away from unsafe areas and mean people.* "Does anyone know where bullies hang out?" You should have the results of the anonymous student questionnaires that identify dangerous locations in and around the school campus. See if the students are able to come up with these places by themselves. If not, review each identified dangerous place with the students.

3. *Tell students not to respond to bullying e-mails, text messages, and phone calls.* "Bullies can also be on the Internet or call you on your phone. Suppose someone calls you, e-mails you, or texts you and calls you names? What's wrong with doing it back to them?" The answer is that the bullying continues and maybe gets worse. Maybe you will get into trouble for answering back. Ask, "What's a better thing to do?" Acceptable answers are "Don't answer back" and "Block their number and tell your parents about it. Keep the message for evidence."

4. *Review Handout 11.1.*

Homework Assignment

Have students ask their parents if they would lose phone or computer privileges if they told their parents that someone was bothering them on the phone or with e-mail. Follow up the next session to see if they asked their parents and what their parents told them.

Assessment

Reductions in bullying reported in retests of online questionnaires will document decreases in bullying and other forms of victimization.

HANDOUT 11.1 How to Protect Your Child Against Cyberbullying

An Internet Web site set up by the federal government (http://www.stopbullying .gov/topics/cyberbullying/parents/index.html) suggests the following steps to protect students from cyberbullying:

WHAT PARENTS CAN DO TO PREVENT AND STOP CYBERBULLYING

- The most common reason children give for not telling their parents they are being bullied is that they are afraid their parents will take away their phone or Internet privileges. Tell your child you would never do this. Never threaten to or actually take away these privileges if your child tells you he or she is being harassed or bullied.

- Set up your child's computers in easily observable areas of the house rather than his or her bedroom.

- Strongly encourage your child not to respond to the cyberbullying.

- If your child is cyberbullied, do not erase the messages or pictures. Save them as evidence. In addition, try to identify the individual doing the cyberbullying. Even if the cyberbully is anonymous (say, using a fake name or someone else's identity), there may be a way to track this person through your Internet service provider.

HOW PARENTS CAN GET HELP IF THEIR CHILD IS A VICTIM OF CYBERBULLYING

- Sending inappropriate language may violate the terms and condi-tions of e-mail services, Internet service providers, Web sites, and cell phone companies. Consider contacting these providers and filing a complaint.

- If the cyberbullying is coming through e-mail or a cell phone, it may be possible to block future contact from the cyberbully. Of course, the cyberbully may assume a different identity and continue the cyberbul-lying.

- If the cyberbullying is occurring through your school district's Internet system, school administrators have an obligation to intervene. Even if the cyberbullying is occurring off campus, make the school adminis-trators aware of the problem. They may be able to help you resolve the cyberbullying or be watchful for face-to-face bullying.

- Consider contacting an attorney in cases of serious cyberbullying. In some circumstances, civil law permits victims to sue a bully or his or her parents in order to recover damages.

HANDOUT 11.1 (continued)

- Contact the police if cyberbullying involves acts such as these:
  - Threats of violence
  - Extortion
  - Obscene or harassing phone calls or text messages
  - Harassment, stalking, or hate crimes
  - Child pornography
  - Sexual exploitation
  - Taking a photo image of someone in a place where he or she would expect privacy

NOTES:

CHAPTER 12

Working with Peer Mentors

In the late 1950s, Robert Edgerton, an anthropologist, studied how forty-eight young adults with mild developmental disabilities adapted in their community. They were hospitalized as children and teens in a California state hospital and discharged as young adults, without any preparation, after experiencing the severe environmental deprivation of the state hospital. Edgerton emphasized their need to deny their cognitive handicap and attempt to pass as normal in society, calling this phenomenon the "cloak of competence." Edgerton found that their social adaptation was substantially better than originally predicted, especially when a community mentor was available to consult in times of crisis.

A mentor is someone who advises, not someone who does something for us. Neither is a mentor a friend because the relationship is inherently unequal. Instead, mentors are people we respect and sometimes are a model for how to lead a successful life. We accept the advice of mentors because they are the experts. They are only peripherally involved in our lives, and we seek their help only when we need it, for mentors are generally volunteers and not to be taken for granted. We don't want to be a burden on them, and we hope that they will be willing to give us help in times of need.

Employing slightly older peer mentors for teens on the spectrum has several advantages. First, since regular education teachers are busy with instructional needs and disciplinary commitments, they have little time to devote to helping an individual student on the spectrum with day-to-day issues. Peer mentors could more readily fill this need. Second, a well-chosen peer mentor can be more intimately aware of the social environment that the adolescents find themselves in. Their advice could be more precise than that given by adults. Third, peer mentorship can be constructed in such a way as to minimize any stigma associated with the extra help. It may be more acceptable to the teen receiving the help and also appear more respectable to other teens observing the process. Fourth, having the student with autism spectrum disorders learn how to use mentors is a viable alternative to depending solely on parents and other family members. The problem with family members is that they are frequently overinvolved and not necessarily as knowledgeable as they should be in relevant social matters. Selecting a peer mentor may better fill this role.

There are limitations to what a peer mentor can do, of course. In practice, it is difficult to give peer mentors enough intervention skills and enough time with mentees to be solely effective in improving the social skills of the teen on the spectrum. Peer mentorship must be viewed as an effective adjunct to evidence-based social skills training and antibullying policies.

This chapter first describes some commonly used alternatives to the peer mentorship and discusses problems they pose. Then it presents a mentorship approach that does not have these shortcomings. This approach has been adapted from the many resources available on the Internet. Such programs have had great success for students with a number of problems other than those associated with autism spectrum disorders.

Commonly Used Alternatives to Mentoring

Three other methods besides mentoring have been used to try to get peers to help students with disabilities in school settings: peer tutoring, peer pairing, and more formal instruction to peer mentors. Each of these approaches has had substantial shortcomings, however. In peer tutoring, the mentor's role is primarily focused on academic instruction. There is little evidence that the student on the spectrum will become friends with the peer tutor or that the peer tutor might facilitate friendships within his friendship circle in any lasting way. Anecdotal accounts suggest that the tutor rarely mixes socially with his pupil outside the tutoring situation.

In peer pairing, a more popular student is paired with an unpopular student. In one study, developmentally disabled children were paired with more popular neurotypical students. In this model, the mentors are not provided with instruction on how to address their mentee's social problems. There were some initial benefits; however, once the pairing stopped, the benefits disappeared.

A third approach is to use socially competent peers as formal instructors in social skills sessions. Two studies using this approach showed that problematic behaviors decreased in the mentees. But the mentees were not socially accepted by their peers after the intervention was completed.

Job Description of the Cross-Age Mentor

We conceive of the ideal peer mentoring arrangement as a relationship between a younger mentee (by at least two years) and an older teen as mentor. Unlike a friendship, a cross-age mentorship is asymmetrical, in that the mentee takes advice and guidance from the mentor and not the reverse. Also the relationship focuses on specific goals. In this case, the older teen helps guide the younger teen's development in interpersonal skills and conventional connectedness. Cross-age mentoring can prevent feelings of inferiority and stigma on the part of the mentee, which can occur when they are mentored or tutored by a student of the same age. Mentors who are older than their mentees can take advantage of the higher status provided by their age difference, but be selected and assigned to mentees on the basis of similarity and compatibility.

An ideal time for mentorship to begin is when the adolescent on the spectrum enters middle school. This school transition is difficult even for many neurotypical students. Students need assistance in settling in with an entirely different kind of schedule from elementary school and learning about middle school life. Thus, mentoring the student on the spectrum can take place when other students are mentored for a host of reasons, further reducing any stigma of being mentored. Examples are students who have just immigrated to the United States or moved from another part of the country, students with some physical disability, and all fully included students who are just beginning middle school. Effective mentoring at this time doesn't give a negative reputation a chance to build up and have to be overcome.

Step 1: Selecting Mentors

The selection process should start with a letter to the mentor's parents after the potential mentor has volunteered (Handout 12.1). For purposes of matching mentor and mentee, potential mentors should fill out an application detailing their academic and social interests and their ethnic and cultural backgrounds, along with a short statement about why they're interested in becoming a mentor. (P. Woody's "Peer-Mentoring for at-Risk Middle School Students," listed in the Resources and References section, offers sample forms.) The form should ask for preferences, if any, in terms of the mentee they are assigned and whether they are interested in working with a mentee who has mild but unusual behaviors (mentioning that they will be trained on how to address these behaviors).

Mentors are chosen because they are academically successful and possess good communication, social, and leadership skills and they are responsible enough to honor a commitment for a year. The ideal mentor is

HANDOUT 12.1 Information for Parents of a Potential Mentor

Dear Parents:

Your child may be interested in volunteering as a peer mentor for a younger student at our school who may have a difficult time adjusting to middle school. Our peer mentoring program is intended to help students integrate better into the social life of our school. The peer mentors develop even more compassion for students with differences in abilities, who can benefit from the gifts and skills that the mentors have. The mentors also get to learn valuable skills to help others.

We would like your permission to invite your child for this important assignment because of his or her reputation for maturity and kindness. Mentorship is a limited commitment. It involves meeting with the mentee once a week and perhaps an occasional phone call. There is also a training session and meetings with the mentee supervisor once per month. Mentors learn how to listen effectively to their mentee's issues and help them solve their own problems. There is a two-week trial period to see if the mentee is a good match. With prior notice, either the mentor or mentee can discontinue this arrangement.

A mentor is not:

- A (surrogate) parent
- A professional counselor or therapist
- A flawless or infallible idol
- A social worker
- A lending institution
- A playmate
- Free after-school care

It is important to emphasize that this is not assigning a friend to a younger student. A mentor is someone the other student can rely on to help him or her better understand and integrate with others who may become friends.

Please let us know if you have questions. If not, please sign the attached consent form if you agree to allow your child to become a mentor.

Sincerely,

well liked, with an interest in helping people and learning about his mentee (see Chapter Two, where we discuss altruistic teens). A mentor should be the same gender and ethnicity as his mentee.

The ideal mentor is socially skilled in the ways of middle school and the crowd most appropriate to the mentee. He is respected by members of that crowd so that he understands how to teach the mentee to approach and fit into that crowd. The crowd is important to the process of defining teen identity, as our experiences with the PEERS intervention have shown us. If the teen on the spectrum might have interests, activities, and social skills adequate to fit into one of these crowds, then the mentor should be familiar with the culture of that crowd and should share many of the same interests. For instance, the mentor may run with the "brains" crowd and the mentee on the spectrum may best fit into the "computer geeks." Nevertheless, in order for the match to be successful, the mentor should have well-developed interests in computers and have hung around with computer geeks. The mentor should not include the mentee into his particular crowd (they are all older anyway), only give pointers about how to fit in with the teen's potential circle.

Step 2: Selecting Mentees

Mentee selection should start with a letter to the parent of potential mentees (see Handout 12.2). The selection process for the mentor program should also apply to mentees. Mentees should be selected on the basis of their conversational skills (see Chapters Five through Seven), their willingness to follow the direction of an older peer, and their responsibility for keeping appointments with the mentor. The issue of diagnosis comes into play here. Parents and teens on the spectrum need to consent to share this with a mentor. Then specific training (see Chapter Two) can be implemented.

Prior parental consent should be obtained with the goals and limitations of the mentorship program laid out in specific detail in the consent form. The sample letter to parents in Handout 12.2 clearly spells out the responsibilities and limitations of the mentor.

The mentee should complete an application form that lists his interests and hobbies and any special considerations the potential mentor should know about. Since the mentor will receive some training around the mentee's diagnosis, this should also be included.

HANDOUT 12.2 Information for Parents of a Student Interested in Being Assigned a Mentor

Dear Parents:

We would like to bring to your attention our mentoring program. The program matches a volunteer seventh or eighth grader to help beginning middle schoolers integrate into the social fabric of our school. Many students have a particularly difficult time with this school transition. If your child is interested, we will try to match your child with a student who has similar interests. Mentors are selected for their reputation for maturity, social skill, and kindness.

After an initial trial period, both mentor and mentee are asked to make a commitment to meet together once a week at a mutually convenient time at school. They will start out with joint activities of mutual interest. The expectations of the peer mentors are limited. It is important to emphasize that this is not assigning a friend to a younger student but someone these younger students can rely on to help them better understand and integrate into middle school life. Mentors also take a pledge of confidentiality.

A mentor is not:

- A (surrogate) parent
- A professional counselor or therapist
- A flawless or infallible idol
- A social worker
- A lending institution
- A playmate
- Free after-school care

Peer mentoring programs are very effective in helping beginning middle schoolers integrate into the social life of the school. If your child is interested in being a mentee, please contact the mentor coordinator at _____.

Sincerely,

Step 3: Mentor Orientation

The orientation session, the most important part of the mentor's training, should occur shortly before meeting the mentee to ensure that the learning will be retained. The orientation should address the goals and purposes of the program, the time and length of commitments, expectations of the individuals, benefits of the program, roles of the participants and their family members, limitations of the program, and the supervisory support provided.

An important part of mentorship is the skill to listen effectively to the mentee's issues before providing any guidance. Therefore, an important part of the mentor's training should be in reflective listening skills. An example of an orientation session is presented in Lesson Plan 12.1. The mentor who is assigned to a teen on the autism spectrum should also become familiar with Lesson Plan 2.1 in order to learn about autism spectrum disorder and have some guidelines about how best to help the mentee.

Step 4: Matching Mentor and Mentee

It is best for the mentorship supervisor to set up an initial meeting with the mentor, the mentee, and the mentee's parents. The meeting should take place in the supervisor's office. During this initial meeting, the mentor and mentee can talk a little about themselves, including their backgrounds and interests. Feedback on this initial meeting can be used to make the final assignment. In addition, a two-week trial period should be in place so that either party can back out of the arrangement. If both want to continue, then it's a good practice to have the mentor, mentee, and mentee's parents sign contracts at this point in which the mentee agrees with these conditions:

- Meeting with the mentor weekly.

- Letting the mentor know in advance of any cancellations and immediately rescheduling them.

- A clause allowing either party to back out of the agreement.

- A clause that the mentor will keep everything said between him and his mentee confidential and to share what the mentee tells him only with the mentee supervisor. The mentor's supervisor may break confidentiality to the mentorship supervisor in case of suspected harm to the mentee or others.

Step 5: The Mentorship Term

After an initial trial period, the mentorship should last for at least a year. The mentor–mentee relationship proceeds in three phases:

Phase 1, the bonding stage when a relationship develops. Meetings with mentees should probably be more frequent at first. At this stage, mentor and mentee should arrange to get together around mutually enjoyable activities that are based on their common interests.

Phase 2, the helping phase, where the mentor does most of the active guidance.

Phase 3, termination as the mentor moves on and the mentee becomes more independent.

The mentor's relationship should be primarily with the mentee, not with the mentee's parents. Mentors should not be viewed as doing the parents' bidding or representing the parent because this would impair the mentor–mentee relationship.

Mentors should be provided with ongoing supervision at least once a month. A supervisor should be available to monitor that the meetings are taking place, answer all questions and provide guidance to the mentor, and be prepared to intervene should any self- or other harm reporting be necessary.

There are many potential rewards for the mentor besides the warm feeling of helping others:

- The mentors gain valuable experience working with students with special needs.

- The arrangement may promote increased understanding of and empathy for students with disabilities.

- Serving as an important role model for another student may enhance the self-esteem of the mentor.

- Mentorship may lead to recommendations to aid college admission.

- Mentors may have special-status access to the principal, teachers, or school psychologist.

- Peer mentoring organizations may set up social events for mentors who participate in the program. These events can include mentor–mentee dinners and "graduation" when the mentor leaves the program at the end of the mentoring year.

Termination is a time for the mentor to reflect on the progress the mentee has made and future possibilities, and whether the mentor and mentee will continue their relationship on an informal basis.

Step 6: Assessment

The objectives of a peer mentoring program should be well defined and measurable. Minimal criteria for effectiveness are that the mentor and mentee meet regularly, the mentee finds the mentor's advice helpful, and the mentor sees his advice taken seriously by the mentee. Rating forms can be given to both parties. Parents can also be given rating forms regarding their impressions of the benefits their child is receiving from the mentor. It is highly recommended that evaluations be given to the mentors and mentees at the middle and end of their experience together. A supervisor should review these evaluations in order to make adjustments to supervision.

LESSON PLAN 12.1 Peer Mentoring Initial Training

SELECTED STUDENT NEED

- Starting middle school is a stressful time for many students. Mentors will learn how they can help a younger student.

LEARNING OBJECTIVES

- Mentors will be trained in their duties and responsibilities to their mentees.
- Mentors will be trained on how to establish a working relationship with their mentees.
- Mentors will be trained on how to set limits on unreasonable mentee behavior.
- Mentors will be trained on how to listen and give advice effectively.

STANDARDS AND BENCHMARKS

- Demonstrate skills for effective listening and advice giving.
- Help the student on the spectrum in conversations and activities.

MATERIALS AND RESOURCES

- Handout 12.3, "What Is a Mentor?"
- Handout 12.4, "Reflective Listening"

Introduction

Start by saying, "You have been selected because you are mature students who honor their commitments. You also have good social skills and want to help others. We think you will be a good match for your mentee because you share a lot of interests, even though you are older."

The Class Session

1. Review the benefits of the program with the mentors:

   - Mentors gain valuable experience working with students with special needs.
   - The arrangement may promote increased understanding and empathy for students with disabilities.
   - Mentorship may lead to recommendations to aid college admission.
   - Mentors may have special-status access to the principal, teachers, or school psychologist.

- Mention any special events such as mentor–mentee dinners and "graduation" when the mentor leaves the program at the end of the mentoring year.

2. Review Handout 12.3, "What Is a Mentor?"

3. Describe the supervisory support that will be provided, including how often and where mentors meet with supervisors.

4. Reflective listening:

   - Break up the mentors into dyads.
   - Review each point of Handout 12.4.
   - Demonstrate each point first by modeling it in a conversation.
   - Have dyads practice each point.

Homework Assignment

Have mentors practice reflective listening with a friend or family member, showing them Handout 12.4 before the practice.

Assessment

The mentor will have a clear idea of job responsibilities and advice-giving techniques as demonstrated by performance in this session.

Social Skills Success for Students with Autism/Asperger's, copyright © 2011 John Wiley and Sons, Inc.

HANDOUT 12.3 What Is a Mentor?

A mentor is someone older and wiser who has earned the respect and trust of his mentee. He takes his mentee under his wing and shows him the ropes. You are your mentee's guide because you have had similar experiences, not because you are all-knowing. If you and your mentee like the match, we expect that you will see your mentee for about a year on a weekly basis.

Jobs of a Mentor

Your first job is to develop a relationship with your mentee. Advice is more easily accepted when a relationship is first developed. You can build a relationship with your mentee by doing activities you both enjoy. Here are some suggestions on how to do this:

- Have fun together.
- Have your mentee pick the activities you do together.
- Let your mentee choose what the two of you talk about.
- Be positive about what he or she is saying.
- Remember that your relationship is with the teen, not the parents.

After several weeks, your mentee should be receptive to guidance you offer. Sometimes mentees start this process by asking for help, and sometimes it is up to the mentor to start this process. When you give advice, you should be casual about it. Space out your advice because too much at once can be overwhelming. You can use your personal experiences (without all the details) such as, "When I was a sixth grader, I used to ..."

The types of help you can offer as a mentor are as follows:

- Help your mentee select the crowd that's closest to his interests; for instance, the jocks if he is athletic, the band crowd if he plays a musical instrument, and the computer geeks if he is knowledgeable about computer software or hardware.
- Help your mentee fit in better with tips on grooming, dress, and hygiene.
- Expand your mentee's interests into related activities where he can make new friends.
- Advise your mentee on safe and dangerous places (and people) on and around campus.
- Teach your mentee rules of behavior—for instance, how to approach others, whom to approach, and Internet safety rules.

HANDOUT 12.3   (continued)

In addition:

- Do not involve your mentee in your personal life or friendships.
- You can be available by phone, but not to the point where it is constant. You can limit the number of phone calls each week if you need to.
- You are allowed to (and should) say no to anything you consider unreasonable. Remember that setting clear boundaries promotes respect.

NOTES:

Social Skills Success for Students with Autism/Asperger's, copyright © 2011 John Wiley and Sons, Inc.

HANDOUT 12.4 Reflective Listening

Many people don't understand that listening is a skill. When you listen effectively, you understand better what someone is trying to tell you. It is an important skill to have when your mentee is asking you for help with a problem. Approach the conversation with the belief that your mentee has the ability to solve the problem for him- or herself.

STEPS OF REFLECTIVE LISTENING

1. At first, **avoid offering advice or giving opinions** about what the mentee is saying. Instead, ask questions such as, "So how will you deal with that?" and "What do you think can or should be done about this situation?"

2. **Paraphrase what your mentee is saying,** repeating the statement in question form. For example, if your mentee said, "They didn't let me into their conversation!" you might reply, "You feel like they weren't open to including you?"

3. **Ask clarifying questions** in order to make sure you understand what your mentee is saying. For example, if your mentee said, "That kid just made me feel so stupid!" you might say, "It sounds as if you're pretty upset. What did he do to make you feel stupid?"

4. Your mentee may not show or recognize emotions. **Listen for the underlying emotion.** For example, if your mentee said, "They didn't let me into their conversation!" you might say, "You sound frustrated."

5. When your mentee is done, **briefly summarize what you think was said.** Ask your mentee if your summary was correct.

Sometimes your mentee may get off topic. Bring him back to his original issue with a statement like, "That's also interesting, but we were talking about [identify the topic]. Let's finish that first before we talk about anything else."

Finally, **do not** try to solve a problem for your mentee without having him or her try first.

CONCLUSION: HELPING KIDS ON THE SPECTRUM FIND THEIR OWN PLACE IN THE WORLD

They see him as quirky cool. I think they really are impressed by his use of big words, his logical approach to everything, his frankness, and his confidence. He always has something to say that's interesting—a new and different viewpoint.

Too often children with autism spectrum disorders are oblivious to positive peer approaches and aren't interested in socializing. However, as teens, many of them wake up to the world around them and want to be part of it. They are eager for a second chance to try to catch up on what they have missed. As you can see from the vignette that starts this chapter, they have a lot to offer their peers if they are able to overcome their anxiety and figure out how to acquire the social knowledge they need to fit in. Integrating tweens and teens with autism spectrum disorders into the fabric of middle and high school life is entirely possible. These adolescents in fact may have a fresh and different viewpoint that their peers may find intriguing. They may be charming and fun to converse with. We hope that this book has provided you with the tools needed to help young people on the spectrum reach social success.

RESOURCES AND REFERENCES

INTRODUCTION

Useful Resources

Frankel, F., & Myatt, R. (2003). *Children's friendship training*. New York: Routledge. This is the original treatment manual describing evidence-based treatment for children with friendship problems. Field-tested now on over fourteen hundred children and subject to numerous research studies on its effectiveness.

Laugeson, E., & Frankel, F. (2010). *Skills for teenagers with developmental and autism spectrum disorders: The PEERS treatment manual*. New York: Routledge. This manual is the adaptation of *Children's Friendship Training* for teens. Also evidence based and tested on teens on the spectrum.

References

Wood, J. J., Drahota, A., & Sze, K. M. (2007). *Behavioral interventions for anxiety in children with autism (BIACA)*. Unpublished intervention manual appendix prepared at UCLA.

Wood, J. J., Ehrenreich, J., & Storch, E. (2010). *Behavioral interventions for anxiety in children with autism (BIACA)*. Unpublished intervention manual appendix prepared at UCLA.

Wood, J. J., & McLeod, B. D. (2008). *Child anxiety disorders: A family-based treatment manual for practitioners*. New York: Norton.

CHAPTER ONE

Useful Resources

Attwood, T. (2008). *The complete guide to Asperger's Syndrome*. Philadelphia: Kingsley. This book should be called the encyclopedia of autism spectrum disorders as it reviews causes and characteristics in a way that is helpful to professionals and parents alike. Attwood is a foremost authority.

References

Baron-Cohen, S. (1989). The autistic child's theory of mind: A case of specific developmental delay. *Journal of Child Psychology and Psychiatry, 30,* 285–297.

Bauminger, N., & Kasari, C. (2000). Loneliness and friendship in high-functioning children with autism. *Society for Research in Child Development, 71,* 447–456.

Eberly, M. B., & Montemayor, R. (1999). Adolescent affection and helpfulness toward parents: A two-year follow-up. *Journal of Early Adolescence, 19,* 226–248.

Emerich, D. M., Creaghead, N. A., Grether, S. M., Murray, D., & Grasha, C. (2003). The comprehension of humorous materials by adolescents with high-functioning autism and Asperger's syndrome. *Journal of Autism and Developmental Disorders, 33,* 253–257.

Gifford-Smith, M. E., & Brownell, C. A. (2003). Childhood peer relationships: Social acceptance, friendships, and peer networks. *Journal of School Psychology, 41,* 235–284.

Montemeyer, R. (1982). The relationships between parent–adolescent conflict and the amount of time adolescents spend alone and with parents and peers. *Child Development, 53,* 1512–1519.

Montemayer, R., & Hanson, E. (1985). A naturalistic view of conflict between adolescents and their parents and siblings. *Journal of Early Adolescence, 5,* 23–30.

Myles, B. S., & Simpson, R. L. (2002). Asperger syndrome: An overview of characteristics. *Focus on Autism and Other Developmental Disabilities, 17,* 132–137.

CHAPTER TWO

Useful Resources

Antonak, R. E., & Larrivee, B. (1995). Psychometric analysis and revision of the opinions relative to mainstreaming scale. *Exceptional Children, 62,*

139–149. A useful measure to assess parent satisfaction with mainstreaming and inclusion.

Carlo, G., Hausmann, A., Christiansen, S., & Randall, B. A. (2003). Sociocognitive and behavioral correlates of a measure of prosocial tendencies for adolescents. *Journal of Early Adolescence, 23,* 107–134. An informative study that reports a measure of altruism for teens and its relationships to other important factors.

Books Helping Teens with Organization

Cooper-Kahn, J., & Dietzel, L. (2008). *Late, lost, and unprepared: A parents' guide to helping children with executive functioning.* Bethesda, MD: Woodbine House.

Dawson, P., & Guare, R. (2009). *Smart but scattered: The revolutionary "executive skills" approach to helping kids reach their potential.* New York: Guilford Press.

Kutscher, M. L., & Moran, M. (2009). *Organizing the disorganized child: Simple strategies to succeed in school.* New York: HarperCollins.

References

Carlo, G., Hausmann, A., Christiansen, S., & Randall, B. A. (2003). Sociocognitive and behavioral correlates of a measure of prosocial tendencies for adolescents. *Journal of Early Adolescence, 23,* 107–134.

Chamberlain, B., Kasari, C., & Rotheram-Fuller, E. (2007). Involvement or isolation? The social networks of children with autism in regular classrooms. *Journal of Autism and Developmental Disorders, 37,* 230–242.

Gallagher, P. A., Floyd, J. H., Stafford, A. M., Taber, T. A., Brozovic, S. A., & Alberto, P. A. (2000). Inclusion of students with moderate or severe disabilities in educational and community settings: Perspectives from parents and siblings. *Education and Training in Mental Retardation and Developmental Disabilities, 35,* 135–147.

Jones, A. P., & Frederickson, N. (2010). Multi-informant predictors of social inclusion for students with autism spectrum disorders attending mainstream school. *Journal of Autism and Developmental Disorders, 40,* 1094–1103.

Kasari, C., Freeman, S., Bauminger, N., & Alkin, M. (1999). Parental perspectives on inclusion: Effects of autism and Down syndrome. *Journal of Autism and Developmental Disorders, 29,* 297–305.

Leyser, Y., & Kirk, R. (2004). Evaluating inclusion: An examination of parent views and factors influencing their perspectives. *International Journal of Disability, Development and Education, 51,* 271–285.

Mesibov, G., & Shea, V. (1996). Full inclusion and students with autism. *Journal of Autism and Developmental Disorders, 26,* 337–346.

Swaim, K. F., & Morgan, S. B. (2001). Children's attitudes and behavioral intentions toward a peer with autistic behaviors: Does a brief educational intervention have an effect? *Journal of Autism and Developmental Disorders, 31,* 195–205.

Thibaut, J. W., & Kelley, H. H. (1959). *The social psychology of groups.* Hoboken, NJ: Wiley.

Vaughn, S., Elbaum, B. E., Schumm, J. S., & Hughes, M. T. (1998). Social outcomes for students with and without learning disabilities in inclusive classrooms. *Journal of Learning Disabilities, 31,* 428–436.

CHAPTER THREE

Useful Resources

Emmer, E. T., & Everston, C. M. (2008). *Classroom management for middle and high school teachers (with MyEducationLab)* (8th ed.). Needham Heights, MA: Allyn & Bacon. A best-selling and comprehensive, but expensive, work detailing many aspects of classroom management.

Sprick, R. S. (2008). *Discipline in the secondary classroom: A positive approach to behavior management, Second Edition.* San Francisco: Jossey-Bass. This book focuses more on discipline and is quite thorough.

CHAPTER FOUR

Reference

Mercier, C., Mottron, L., & Belleville, S. (2000). A psychosocial study on restricted interests in high functioning persons with pervasive developmental disorders. *Autism, 4,* 406–425.

CHAPTER FIVE

Useful Resources

Ammer, C. (2003). *The American heritage dictionary of idioms.* Boston: Houghton Mifflin Harcourt. Reference books on slang suffer from the problem of considerable delay between when a new slang word is being used and when it finally appears in a revised dictionary. Probably more useful to older teenagers are smartphone applications that are updated more frequently and teens can use almost immediately after they hear an expression that they don't understand. Here are two examples of current applications on popular smartphones:

iPhone app: http://download.famouswhy.com/american_idioms
   _dictionary_iphone_ipad_/

Android app: http://www.pocketgear.com/en/usd/11611,HTC
   -Wildfire/6397141,product-details,American-Idioms-Dictionary
   -Android.html

Although most schools prohibit the use of phones during school hours, they can be used in extracurricular activities and social events.

Commonly used American slang: http://www.manythings.org/slang/. An easy-to-use interface that makes it easy for the teen to quiz himself while learning more important slang expressions.

Dave's ESL café: http://www.eslcafe.com/idioms/id-mngs.html. A large collection of idioms for ESL learners with meanings and sample sentences.

References

Ackerman, B. R. (1982). Contextual integration and utterance interpretation: The ability of children and adults to interpret sarcastic utterances. *Child Development, 53,* 1075–1083.

Capelli, C. A., Nakagawa, N., & Madden, C. (1990). How children understand sarcasm: The role of context and intonation. *Child Development, 61,* 1824–1842.

Creusere, M. A. (1999). Theories of adults' understanding and use of irony and sarcasm: Applications to and evidence from research with children. *Developmental Review, 19,* 213–262.

Ford, J. A., & Milosky, L. M. (1997). The role of prosody in children's inferences of ironic intent. *Discourse Processes, 23,* 47–62.

Glenwright, M., & Pexman, P. M. (2010). Development of children's ability to distinguish sarcasm and verbal irony. *Journal of Child Language, 37,* 429–451.

Harris, M., & Pexman, P. M. (2003). Children's perceptions of the social functions of verbal irony. *Discourse Processes, 36,* 147–165.

McDonald, S. (1999). Exploring the process of inference generation in sarcasm: A review of normal and clinical studies. *Brain and Language, 68,* 486–506.

Morton, J. B., & Trehub, S. E. (2001). Children's understanding of emotion in speech. *Child Development, 72,* 834–843.

Roberts, R. M., & Kreuz, R. J. (1994). Why do people use figurative language? *Psychological Science, 5,* 159–163.

Sigelman, C. K., & Davis, P. J. (1978). Making good impressions in job interviews: Verbal and nonverbal predictors. *Education and Training of the Mentally Retarded, 13,* 71–77.

Winner, E., Levy, J., Kaplan, J., & Rosenblatt, E. (1988). Children's understanding of nonliteral language. *Journal of Aesthetic Education, 22,* 51–63.

CHAPTER SIX

Useful Resource

Landa, R., Piven, J., Wzorek, M., Gayle, J., Chase, G., & Folstein, S. (1992). Social language use in parents of autistic individuals. *Psychological Medicine, 22,* 245–254. Presents the Pragmatic Rating Scale, a language assessment specifically geared to detect language problems of students with autism spectrum disorders. Using this tool may help to assess strengths and deficits in language product and conversation.

References

Cho, E. H., & Larke, P. J. (2010). Repair strategies usage of primary elementary ESL students: Implications for ESL teachers. *TESL-EJ, 14,* 1–18. http://tesl-ej.org/pdf/ej55/a4.pdf.

Hirst, G., McRoy, S., Heeman, P., Edmonds, P., & Horton, D. (1994). Repairing conversational misunderstandings and non-understandings. *Speech Communication, 15,* 213–229.

Todman, J., & Alm, N. (1997). Pragmatics and AAC approaches to conversational goals. In A. Copestake, S. Langer, & S. Palazuelos-Cagigas (Eds.), *Natural language processing for communication aids: Proceedings of a workshop sponsored by the Association for Computational Linguistics* (pp. 1–7). Madrid: Association for Computational Linguistics.

CHAPTER EIGHT

Useful Resource

Daniel, L. S., & Billingsley, B. S. (2010). What boys with an autism spectrum disorder say about establishing and maintaining friendships. *Focus Autism and Other Developmental Disabilities.* doi:10.1177/1088357610378290. Interviews with teens on the spectrum about their strategies for making friends.

References

Bauminger, N., & Shulman, C. (2003). The development and maintenance of friendship in high-functioning children with autism. *Autism, 7,* 81–97.

Bauminger, N., Shulman, C., & Agam, G. (2003). Peer interaction and loneliness in high-functioning children with autism. *Journal of Autism and Developmental Disorders, 33,* 489–507.

Bauminger, N., Solomon, M., Aviezer, A., Heung, K., Brown, J., & Rogers, S. (2008). Friendship in high-functioning children with autism spectrum disorder: Mixed and non-mixed dyads. *Journal of Autism and Developmental Disorders, 38,* 1211–1229.

Bauminger, N., Solomon, M., & Rogers, S. J. (2010). Predicting friendship quality in autism spectrum disorders and typical development. *Journal of Autism and Developmental Disorders, 40,* 751–761.

Daniel, L. S., & Billingsley, B. S. (2010). What boys with an autism spectrum disorder say about establishing and maintaining friendships. *Focus Autism and Other Developmental Disabilities.* doi:10.1177/1088357610378290.

Nelson, J., & Aboud, F. E. (1985). The resolution of social conflict between friends. *Child Development, 56*, 1009–1017.

Orsmond, G. I., Krauss, M. W., & Seltzer, M. M. (2004). Peer relationships and social and recreational activities among adolescents and adults with autism. *Journal of Autism and Developmental Disorders, 34*, 245–256.

Ozonoff, S., Garcia, N., Clark, E., & Lainhart, J. E. (2005). MMPI-2 Personality Profiles of high-functioning adults with autism spectrum disorders. *Assessment, 12*, 86–95.

CHAPTER NINE

Useful Resource

Birmaher, B., Khetarpal, S., Brent, D., Cully, M., Balach, L., Kaufman, J., et al. (1997). The Screen for Child Anxiety Related Emotional Disorders (SCARED): Scale construction and psychometric characteristics. *Journal of the American Academy of Child and Adolescent Psychiatry, 36*, 545–553. This is a short assessment of anxiety that we have found useful to evaluate outcome of our interventions.

Reference

American Psychological Association. (2004). *Diagnostic and statistical manual of mental disorders* (4th ed.). Washington, DC: Author.

CHAPTER ELEVEN

Useful Resource

Reynolds, W. M. (2003). *Bully victimization: Reynolds Scales For Schools manual.* San Antonio TX: Psychological Corporation. Readily available self-report scales for bullying.

References

Bollmer, J., Milich, R., Harris, M., & Maras, M. (2005). A friend in need: The role of friendship quality as a protective factor in peer victimization and bullying. *Journal of Interpersonal Violence, 20,* 701–712.

Boulton, M. J., & Smith, P. K. (1994). Bully/victim problems in middle-school children: Stability, self-perceived competence, peer perceptions and peer acceptance. *British Journal of Developmental Psychology, 12,* 315–329. http://rse.sagepub.com/content/early/2010/02/18/0741932510361247.

Haynie, D. L., Nansel, T., Eitel, P., Crump, A. D., Saylor, K., Yu, K., et al. (2001). Bullies, victims, and bully/victims: Distinct groups of at-risk youth. *Journal of Early Adolescence, 21,* 29–49.

Heinrichs, R. R. (2003). A whole-school approach to bullying: Special considerations for children with exceptionalities. *Intervention in School and Clinic, 38,* 195–204.

Hodges, E., Boivin, M., Vitaro, F., & Bukowski, W. (1999). The power of friendship: Protection against an escalating cycle of peer victimization. *Developmental Psychology, 5,* 94–101.

Limber, S. P. (2003). Efforts to address bullying in U.S. schools. *American Journal of Health Education, 34,* s23-s29.

Rose, C. A., Monda-Amaya, L. E., & Espelage, D. L. (2010). Bullying perpetration and victimization in special education: A review of the literature. *Remedial and Special Education.* http://rse.sagepub.com/content/32/2/114.full.pdf+html.

Smith, P. K., Mahdavi, J., Carvalho, M., Fisher, S., Russell, S., & Tippett, N. (2008). Cyberbullying: Its nature and impact in secondary school pupils. *Journal of Child Psychology and Psychiatry, 49,* 376–385.

CHAPTER TWELVE

Useful Resources

Garringer, M., & MacRae, P. (2008). *Building effective peer mentoring programs in schools: An introductory guide.* Folsom, CA: Mentoring Resource

Center. http://educationnorthwest.org/webfm_send/169. A nicely organized and complete guide for setting up mentoring programs in schools.

Jucovy, L., & Garringer, M. (2007). *The ABCs of school-based mentoring: Effective strategies for providing quality youth mentoring in schools and communities.* Washington, DC: Hamilton Fish Institute on School and Community Violence. Based on research and best practices of school-based mentoring, this pamphlet presents the basics of setting up a school-based mentoring program.

U.S. Department of Education Mentoring Web site: http://www.edmentoring .org/online_res.html. Provides extensive information on training mentors, doing background checks, and getting community buy-in.

Woody, P. (2009). *Peer-mentoring for at-risk middle school students: A suggested program for North Pole Middle School.* Unpublished doctoral dissertation, University of Alaska Fairbanks. http://www.uaf.edu /apache/educ/graduate/renes_projects/Woodyprojectfinal.pdf. This dissertation reviews setting up a mentoring program for at-risk middle school students at North Pole Middle School in Fairbanks, Alaska. Detailed and extensive materials are also included.

References

Edgerton, R. B. (1993). *The cloak of competence.* Berkeley: University of California Press.

Garringer, M. (2010). Planning a school-based mentoring program. *Lessons Learned, 1,* 1–4.

Middleton, H., Zollinger, J., & Keene, R. (1986). Popular peers as change agents for the socially neglected child in the classroom. *Journal of School Psychology, 24,* 343–350.

INDEX

A

Absence, from school, 128, 136

Accountability, for test scores, 32

Accuracy checks: description of, 90; in social conversations, 101; tips for success in, 96*h*

Achievement, students' worries and, 132–133

Adrenaline, 125, 149

African American Awareness Club, 205

Aides, 30–31

Alternative educational placements. *See* Educational placements

Altruism: lesson in, 39–40*l*; teaching tolerance and, 37; teens' development of, 37–38

American Psychological Association, 129

Anger management, 197

Anxiety: assessment of, 135–138, 139–146*h*; causes of, 8, 124–125; clinical levels of, 125–126; consequences of, 126–129; coping with, 24, 26; and friendships, 24; partial inclusion and, 45; physiological response to, 125, 149; poor management of, 6; recreational interests and, 58; substance abuse and, 126; symptoms of, 125, 135, 136; types of, 129–134

Anxiety disorders, prevalence of, 24, 26, 124

Anxiety, interventions for: effectiveness of teachers in, 148–149; features of, 6–7; foundation of, 149–150; lesson plans for, 155, 156–185*l*; phases of, 150; rewards in, 154; skill building in, 150–154, 156–180*l*; skill practice in, 154, 180–185*l*; small-group approach to, 149; whole-class approach to, 148

Anxious avoidance, 131

Appearance, personal, 133

Applications, for mentors, 214

Assessments: of anxiety, 135–138, 139–146*h*; of mentoring programs, 220; of peer acceptance, 192; to prevent bullying,

201–202; of recreational interests, 59–62, 63*h*; of teens' friendships, 33

Association for Behavioral and Cognitive Therapy, 137

Autism Society of America, 38, 40*l*

Autism spectrum disorders: central deficits of, 3; challenges of teens facing, 14–18; description of, 8, 41–42*h*; parents' instruction to others about, 36–37; prevalence of, 2, 41*h*; symptoms of, 18–26

Autonomy, of teens, 14, 15

B

Behavior modification training, 32

Behavioral challenges: classroom management techniques for, 47–48; as consideration in placement of teens, 34–35; emotional self-regulation and, 6; of neurotypical teens *versus* teens with autism spectrum disorder, 14–15; in regular education classes, 2–3; as response to stress, 128–129; separation anxiety and, 134; social anxiety and, 128–129; success of inclusion and, 34

Best friends: benefits of, 110–111; definition of, 110; importance of, 18; number of teens with, 17, 18

Body language. *See* Nonverbal communication

Bonding, 133–134

Boys: bullying by, 191; communication deficits of, 20; eye contact of, 88; independence of, from parents, 14; intimacy of, 18

Bullying: consequences for, 203; definition of, 190; description of, 190–191, 192–194; effective interventions for, 198–206; friend selection and, 115; ineffective school interventions for, 197–198, 200; legal issues regarding, 195–196; lesson plans to address, 207–208*l*; number of students suffering from, 192, 194–195; online types of, 194–197, 205–206, 209–210*h*; ostracism